KIDS

LOVE

Happy Exploring! George

KENTUCKY

A PARENT'S GUIDE TO EXPLORING FUN PLACES IN KENTUCKY WITH CHILDREN. . .YEAR ROUND!

Kids Love Publications
7438 Sawmill Road, #500
Columbus, OH 43235

www.kidslovepublications.com

**WEST CLINTON
MENNONITE CHURCH**

02/03-09

Dedicated to the Families
of Kentucky

ISBN# 09663457-5-4

KIDS ♥ KENTUCKY ™   Kids Love Publications

MISSION STATEMENT

At first glance, you may think that this is a book that just lists hundreds of places to travel. While it is true that we've invested thousands of hours of exhaustive research (*and drove nearly 3000 miles in Kentucky*) to prepare this travel resource…just listing places to travel is not the mission statement of these projects.

As children, Michele and I were able to travel extensively throughout the United States. We consider these family times some of the greatest memories we cherish today. We, quite frankly, felt that most children had this opportunity to travel with their family as we did. However, as we became adults and started our own family, we found that this wasn't necessarily the case. We continually heard friends express several concerns when deciding how to spend "quality" and "quantity" family time. 1) What to do? 2) Where to do it? 3) How much will it cost? 4) How do I know that my kids will enjoy it?

Interestingly enough, as we compare our experiences with our families when we were kids, many of our fondest memories were not made at an expensive attraction, but rather when it was least expected.

It is our belief and mission statement that if you as a family will study and use the contained information to create family memories, these memories will grow a stronger, tighter family. Our ultimate mission statement is, that your children will develop a love and a passion for quality family experiences that they can pass to another generation of family travelers.

We thank you for purchasing this book, and we hope to see you on the road (*and hearing your travel stories!*) God bless your journeys and happy exploring!

George, Michele, Jenny and Daniel

INTRODUCTION

HOW TO USE THIS BOOK

If you are excited about discovering Kentucky, this is the book for you and your family! We've spent over a thousand hours doing all the scouting, collecting and compiling (*and most often visiting!*) so that you could spend less time searching and more time having fun.

Here are a few hints to make your adventures run smoothly:

- ❏ Consider the **child's age** before deciding to take a visit.
- ❏ Know **directions** and parking. Call ahead (or visit the company's website) if you have questions *and* bring this book. Also, don't forget your camera! *(please honor rules regarding use).*
- ❏ **Estimate the duration** of the trip. Bring small surprises (favorite juice boxes) and travel books and toys.
- ❏ Call ahead for **reservations** or details, if necessary.
- ❏ Most listings are **closed major holidays** unless noted.
- ❏ Make a **family "treasure chest"**. Decorate a big box or use an old popcorn tin. Store memorabilia from a fun outing, journals, pictures, brochures and souvenirs. Once a year, look through the "treasure chest" and reminisce.
- ❏ Plan **picnics** along the way. Many Historical Society sites and state parks are scattered throughout Kentucky. Allow time for a rural/scenic route to take advantage of these free picnic facilities.
- ❏ Some activities, especially tours, require **groups** of 10 or more. To participate, you may either ask to be part of another tour group or get a group together yourself (neighbors, friends, school organizations). If you arrange a group outing, most places offer discounts.

- ❑ For the latest updates corresponding to the pages in this book, visit our website: **www.kidslovepublications.com**.
- ❑ Each chapter represents an area of the state (*see map below*). Each listing is further identified by city, zip code, and place/event name. **The front index lists places by Activity Heading (i.e. Kentucky History, Tours, Outdoors, Museums, etc.), the back index is alphabetical.**

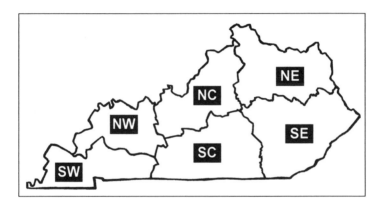

In a Hundred Years...

It will not matter, The size of my bank account...
The kind of house that I lived in, the kind of car
that I drove... But what will matter is...
That the world may be different
Because I was important in the life of a child.

- author unknown

Acknowledgements

We are most thankful to be blessed with our parents, Barbara Darrall and George and Catherine Zavatsky who helped us every way they could – proofing, babysitting, and inspiring family travel when we were children. More importantly, they were great sounding boards and offered loving, unconditional support. Our own young kids, Jenny and Daniel, were delightful and fun children during all of our trips across the state.

We also want to express our sincere thanks to Marge Bateman and the Kentucky Department of Travel for providing the special attention to detail that helps to make this project so successful. We felt very welcome during our extensive travels in Kentucky and would be proud to call it home!

We both sincerely thank each other – our partnership has created a great "marriage of minds" with lots of exciting moments and laughs woven throughout. Above all, we praise the Lord for His many answered prayers and special blessings throughout the completion of this project.

We think Kentucky is a wonderful, friendly area of the country with more activities than you could imagine! Our sincere wish is that this book will help everyone "fall in love" with Kentucky!

"Where to go?, What to do?, and How much will it cost?", are all questions that they have heard throughout the years from friends and family. These questions became the inspiration that motivated them to research, write and publish the "Kids Love" travel series.

This adventure of writing and publishing family travel books has taken them on a journey of experiences that they never could have imagined. They have appeared as guests on over 70 radio and television shows, had featured articles in statewide newspapers and magazines, spoken to thousands of people at schools and conventions, and write monthly columns in many publications talking about "family friendly" places to travel.

George Zavatsky and Michele (Darrall) Zavatsky were raised in the Midwest and have lived in many different cities. They currently reside in a suburb of Columbus, Ohio. They feel very blessed to be able to create their own career that allows them to research, write and publish a series of best-selling kids' travel books. Besides the wonderful adventure of marriage, they place great importance on being loving parents to Jenny and Daniel.

GENERAL INFORMATION

- Canoe Kentucky (800) K-CANOE -1 or www.canoeky.com
- Kentucky Arts Council www.kyarts.org
- Kentucky Bicycle Tours (800) 225-8747
- Kentucky Division of Water (502) 564-3410
- Kentucky River Information Center (859) 527-3131
- Kentucky Roadside Farm Markets www.kyfb.com/roadside.htm
- **Kentucky Tourism Council - www.kytourism.com**
- Kentucky Trails Guide (800) 225-8747
- Lake Cumberland & Big South Fork Area (800) 642-6287
- Louisville MetroParks & Recreation (502) 456-8100
- Oldham County Parks (502) 222-5933
- Winter Indoor Polo, Polo at the Park, KY Horse Park (859) 254-5667

FERRY SERVICES

NE - <u>ANDERSON FERRY</u> - **Florence**, KY 8. Crosses Ohio River to US 50 in Ohio. Hours 6:00am-8:00pm (November-April) and 6:00am-9:30pm (May-October). Open 7:00am on Sundays and holidays. Fare: $3.00 per car.

NE - <u>VALLEY VIEW FERRY</u> - **Nicholasville**, KY 169E at the KY River. The oldest continuous business in KY since 1785. FREE.

NW - <u>CAVE IN ROCK FERRY</u> - **Marion**, KY 91. Crosses the Ohio River to Illinois. FREE

SC - <u>CUMBERLAND RIVER FERRY</u> - **Tompkinsville**, KY 214. Kentucky's only state-operated ferry running 24 hours a day to scenic Turkey Neck Bend.

SW - HICKMAN-DORENA FERRY - **Hickman**, Off KY 94. Ferry crosses the Mississippi river from Hickman to Dorena, MO. Runs daily except Christmas. 7:00am-6:15pm (April-October), 7:00am-5:00pm (November-March). Fare $8.00 per car.

STATE NATURE PRESERVES

- ❑ Phone: (502) 573-2886
  Web: www.nr.state.ky.us/nrepc/dnr/ksnpc/index.htm
- ❑ Hours: Dawn to dusk, daily.
- ❑ Admission: FREE
- ❑ Miscellaneous: Open to the public for hiking, birding & nature study.

NC - VERNON-DOUGLAS STATE NATURE PRESERVE - **Elizabethtown**, off KY 583. Mature second growth forest with rich array of spring wildflowers.

NC - BEARGRASS CREEK STATE NATURE PRESERVE at the Louisville Nature Center - **Louisville**, 1297 Trevilian Way. (502) 458-1328. Over 40 acres of mature forest, adjacent to Creason Park, popular for birding in an urban setting.

NE - BOONE COUNTY CLIFFS STATE NATURE PRESERVE - **Burlington**,   I-75 to KY 18 west. 20 to 40 foot cliffs formed from the gravel washed out of melting glaciers north of the area can be seen.

NE - DINSMORE WOODS STATE NATURE PRESERVE - **Burlington**, I-75 exit 181 to KY 18 west. Park at Middle Creek Park. Fairly undisturbed old growth mixed hardwood forest which hosts various spring wildflowers.

NE - QUIET TRAILS STATE NATURE PRESERVE - **Cynthiana**, off Pugh's Ferry Road, near Sunrise, on the Licking river. Diverse birds, trees and wildflowers, over 20 species of mussels come from the river.

STATE NATURE PRESERVES (cont.)

NE - JESSE STUART STATE NATURE PRESERVE - **Greenup**, West Hollow Road, off KY 1. Known as W-Hollow, it was home to the internationally known author, Jesse Stuart.

NE - JIM BEAM NATURE PRESERVE - **Nicholasville**, US 27 to Hall Lane (near Camp Nelson) to Payne Lane. Protecting a portion of the Palisades of the KY River, this is a feeding habitat for rare bat species.

NE - SALLY BROWN NATURE PRESERVE - **Nicholasville**, US 27 to KY 1845 west to Camp Dick Fire Station left to High Bridge Road right to Bowman's Road right. Protects forests and 400 plant species in the KY River Palisades.

NE - TOM DORMAN STATE NATURE PRESERVE - **Nicholasville**, US 27S to KY 1845. Forested slopes of spring wildflowers on spectacular 300 foot cliffs across the KY River.

SE - BAD BRANCH STATE NATURE PRESERVE - **Whitesburg**, KY 932. Over 1000 acres of forested gorge containing a 60 foot waterfall, rare plants and animals.

SW - LOGAN COUNTY-GLADE STATE NATURE PRESERVE - **Russellville**, off US 68/KY 80. Over 40 acres with limestone glades and a 810 foot knob. The rocky slopes are adorned with prairie grasses and rare plants like Carolina Larkspur, Glade violet and Fame flower.

SW - METROPOLIS LAKE STATE NATURE PRESERVE - **Paducah**, off KY 996. Find five species of rare fish, beaver wintering place for balk eagles with a lake ringed with balk cypress and swamp tupelo.

KENTUCKY DEPARTMENT OF FISH AND WILDLIFE RESOURCES

- ❑ Activity: General Information
- ❑ Phone: (502) 564-4336 or (800) 858-1549
  Web: www.kdfwr.state.ky.us

NC - <u>FRANKFORT FISH HATCHERY</u> - **Frankfort**, Indian Gap Road, north off US 127 near Swallowfield. 45 rearing ponds, hatching house, and feed office occupy the land where fish are raised to stock farm ponds and public lakes and for research.

NE - <u>CAMP ROBERT WEBB CONSERVATION EDUCATION CENTER</u> - **Grayson**. 460 acres of deer and turkey. Vehicle traffic only. Year round Monday-Friday 8:00am-4:00pm.

NW - <u>SLOUGHS PUBLIC WILDLIFE AREA</u> - **Henderson**, Sauerheber Unit, on KY 268 northwest of Geneva. Almost 2000 acres where up to 30,000 Canada geese and 10,000 ducks winter annually, with an observation platform. KY's largest great blue heron rookery. Open mid-March to mid-October.

SW - <u>CAMP JOHN CURRIE CONSERVATION EDUCATION CENTER</u> - **Benton**, US 68 east on KY 962. Children's conservation camp June-August.

Check out these businesses / services in your area for tour ideas:

AIRPORTS

All children love to visit the airport! Why not take a tour and understand all the jobs it takes to run an airport. Tour the terminal, baggage claim, gates and security / currency exchange. Maybe you'll even get to board a plane.

ANIMAL SHELTERS

Great for the would-be pet owner. Not only will you see many cats and dogs available for adoption, but a guide will show you the clinic and explain the needs of a pet. Be prepared to have the children "fall in love" with one of the animals while they are there!

BANKS

Take a "behind the scenes" look at automated teller machines, bank vaults and drive-thru window chutes. You may want to take this tour and then open a savings account for your child.

ELECTRIC COMPANY / POWER PLANTS

Modern science has created many ways to generate electricity today, but what really goes on with the "flip of a switch". Because coal can be dirty, wear old, comfortable clothes. Coal furnaces heat water, which produces steam, that propels turbines, that drive generators, that make electricity.

FIRE STATIONS

Many Open Houses in October, Fire Prevention Month. Take a look into the life of the firefighters servicing your area and try on their gear. See where they hang out, sleep and eat. Hop aboard a real-life fire engine truck and learn fire safety too.

HOSPITALS

Some Children's Hospitals offer pre-surgery and general tours.

NEWSPAPERS

You'll be amazed at all the new technology. See monster printers and robotics. See samples in the layout department and maybe try to put together your own page. After seeing a newspaper made, most companies give you a free copy (dated that day) as your souvenir. National Newspaper Week is in October.

RESTAURANTS

DOMINO'S PIZZA

❑ Various locations

Telephone your local shop for tour status. Free. Usually ages 4+. Takes 15 – 20 minutes. Your children can be pizza bakers! While the group is instructed on ingredients and pizza secrets, they will get to make their own special pizza. After the custom made pizza bakes, your tour guide will take it out of the special oven, box it up and you get to take it home.

PIZZA HUT

❑   Many participating restaurants

Telephone the store manager. Best days are Monday, Tuesday and Wednesday mid-afternoon. Minimum of 10 people. $3.50 per person. All children love pizza – especially when they can create their own! As the children tour the kitchen, they learn how to make a pizza, bake it, and then eat it. The admission charge includes lots of creatively make pizzas, beverage and coloring book.

MCDONALD'S RESTAURANTS

❑   Participating locations

Telephone the store manager. They prefer Monday or Tuesday. Free. What child doesn't love McDonald's food? This is your child's chance to go behind the counter and look at the machines that make all the fun food. You will be shown the freezer and it's alarm, the fryer and hamburger flipping on the grills. There is a free snack at the end of the tour.

SUPERMARKETS

Kids are fascinated to go behind the scenes of the same store where Mom and Dad shop. Usually you will see them grind meat, walk into large freezer rooms, watch cakes and bread bake and receive free samples along the way. Maybe you'll even get to pet a live lobster!

TV / RADIO STATIONS

Studios, newsrooms, Fox kids clubs. Why do weathermen never wear blue clothes on TV? What makes a "DJ's" voice sound so deep and smooth?

WATER TREATMENT PLANTS

A giant science experiment! You can watch seven stages of water treatment. The favorite is usually the wall of bright buttons flashing as workers monitor the different processes.

U.S. MAIN POST OFFICES

Did you know Ben Franklin was the first Postmaster General (over 200 years ago)? Most interesting is the high-speed automated mail processing equipment. Learn how to address envelopes so they will be sent quicker (there are secrets). To make your tour more interesting, have your children write a letter to themselves and address it with colorful markers. Mail it earlier that day and they will stay interested trying to locate their letter in all the high-speed machinery.

COURT WATCHING

Call for an agenda of trials (docket info.) for the following: Common Pleas, Small Claims, Municipal, Domestic/Juvenile. See the Government Section or Community Services of your local White Pages. Did you know as citizens we have the right to enter a courtroom to observe (*except in special cases when a "Do Not Disturb" sign warns otherwise*). Watching trials in session can be wonderful exposure to our legal system, especially for children who have studied law and government. Be sure your children have self-control before planning your visit.

CITY INDEX (Listed by City & Area)

CITY INDEX (Listed by City & Area)

Index by Activity *(Area, City, Place/Event Name, Page)*

AMUSEMENTS

ANIMALS & FARMS

KENTUCKY HISTORY

Index by Activity *(Area, City, Place/Event Name, Page)*

Index by Activity (Area, City, Place/Event Name, Page)

Index by Activity *(Area, City, Place/Event Name, Page)*

THE ARTS (cont.)

THEME RESTAURANTS

TOURS

Table of Contents

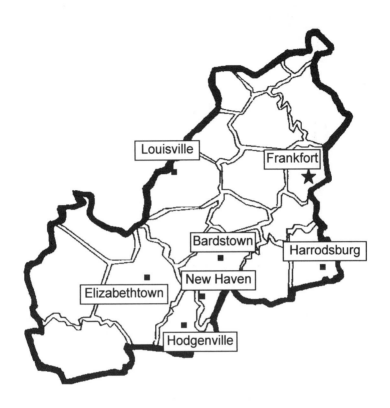

Chapter 1
North Central Area

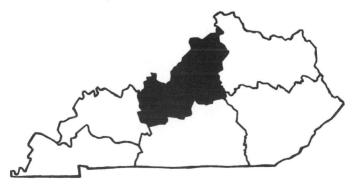

Our Favorites...

- ✓ <u>Civil War Museum</u> – Bardstown
- ✓ <u>My Old Kentucky Home</u> - Bardstown
- ✓ <u>Kentucky History Center</u> – Frankfort
- ✓ <u>Rebecca Ruth Candy</u> – Frankfort
- ✓ <u>Salato Wildlife Educ. Ctr</u>. – Frankfort
- ✓ <u>Legend of Daniel Boone, Old Ft. Harrod State Park</u> – Harrodsburg
- ✓ <u>Lincoln Birthplace</u> – Hodgenville
- ✓ <u>Amer. Printing House/Blind</u> – Louisville
- ✓ <u>Belle of Louisville</u> - Louisville
- ✓ <u>Louisville Slugger Museum</u> – Louisville
- ✓ <u>Pottery Tours</u> – Louisville
- ✓ <u>Kentucky Railway Museum</u> – New Haven

BARDSTOWN TOURMOBILE

107 East Stephen Foster Avenue (Tourist & Convention Commission)

Bardstown 40004

- ❑ Activity: Tours
- ❑ Phone: (502) 348-4877 or (800) 638-4877
  Web: www.bardstowntourism.com
- ❑ Admission: FREE
- ❑ Tours: Monday-Saturday at 9:30am, 10:45am, 1:00pm and 2:15pm (June-August)

The tourmobile leaves from the commission for a 45 minute trip offering an introduction to the town. Families can opt to not stop at the Distillery on weekdays. This is a good way to get oriented to the area before you explore on your own and the staff are very welcoming.

CIVIL WAR MUSEUM

310 East Broadway

Bardstown 40004

- ❑ Activity: Museums
- ❑ Phone: (502) 349-0291, **Web: www.bardstowntourism.com**
- ❑ Hours: (March-December), Monday-Saturday 10:00am-5:00pm, Sunday Noon-5:00pm. Rest of Year, weekends only. Closed New Years, Thanksgiving, and Christmas
- ❑ Admission: $5.00 adults, $4.00 seniors (62+), $2.50 children (7-15)
- ❑ Miscellaneous: The Women in Civil War Museum is just up the street and operated by the same folks. Learn why early nurses were only nuns or plain spinsters; learn why women were the ones to realize more sanitary conditions were needed (famous Clara Barton, Elizabeth Blackwell); and especially learn why women were the best spies! Pioneer Village is next door with authentic cabins. Separate small admission for self-guided tours of either of these other facilities.

See artifacts and photographs from Civil War battles fought in Georgia, Kentucky, Tennessee, Mississippi and Missouri. Also see rare flags, uniforms, maps, both North and South weapons and medical equipment. Trace the progression of the war, chronologically (easy to follow). The also have a campsite featuring a wagon actually used during the conflict on a battlefield. Here's some questions to answer when you tour: Why did West Virginia form as a separate state because of the Civil War? The book "Uncle Tom's Cabin" came out before the war started - did the author start the war? If you were a captain, how many buttons would you wear? Red, Yellow or Blue trim on a uniform - what does it mean? Injured in the war? (be careful, they loved to amputate) Cheer, Boys, Cheer! Would you want to be a drummer boy? Before you leave, be sure to ask the story about the US belt buckle turned upside down. This museum was voted the 4th best Civil War museum in the nation.

MY OLD KENTUCKY HOME STATE PARK

US 150 east of downtown (Bluegrass Pkwy.)

Bardstown 40004

❑   Activity: Museums
❑   Phone: (800) 626-1563, **Web: www.stephenfoster.com**
❑   Hours: (June August), Daily 8:30am-6:30pm; (September-May) Daily 9:00am-4:45pm. Closed major winter holidays.
❑   Admission: $4.50 adults, $4.00 seniors (62+), $2.50 children (6-12)
❑   Miscellaneous: Gift shop, picnic, playground. Tours every fifteen minutes.

The stately Georgian Colonial mansion is most famous because it is the inspiration for Stephen Foster's famous ballad "My Old Kentucky Home" - the official KY state song. It was the home of Judge John Rowan whose Pittsburgh cousin, Stephen Foster, visited in 1852. Visit the days of the antebellum South as costumed guides escort you through the restored mansion, formal gardens, carriage house and smokehouse. Here are some unique things for the kids to look for while on tour: 13 foot high and 13 inch thick walls, 13 windows and 13 steps because of the 13 original colonies; see the "napping couch and Day Bed"; look for the "hip bath" for bathing in the kids' rooms; learn why children ate upstairs in the hallway; or look for the picture that follows you.

OLD TALBOTT TAVERN

107 West Stephen Foster Avenue (Court Square)

Bardstown 40004

- ❑ Activity: Theme Restaurant
- ❑ Phone: (800) 4-TAVERN
- ❑ Hours: Lunch and Dinner daily.
- ❑ Miscellaneous: Bed & Breakfast and Gift Shop. Just browse if you like.

Mid-America's oldest stagecoach stop where historic recipe meals are still served today. It's the oldest inn (1779) in continuous operation located west of the Alleghenies. Notables such as Louis Phillippe, John Audubon, and George Rogers Clark rested here on their journeys and you can see bullet holes shot by Jesse James! Choose from Fried Green Tomatoes, Burgoo, Mrs. Eleanor's Fried Chicken or Country Ham. Although it's historic, it's unusually very kid-friendly. Wait staff are dressed in period and there's a great, fun children's menu.

STEPHEN FOSTER - THE MUSICAL

US 150 east of downtown (Bluegrass Pkwy. On grounds of "My Old Kentucky Home")

Bardstown 40004

- ❑ Activity: The Arts
- ❑ Phone: (800) 626-1563, **Web: www.stephenfoster.com**
- ❑ Hours: (mid-June-Labor Day), Tuesday-Sunday 8:00pm nightly (outdoor theatre, indoors if inclement weather). Saturday matinees at 2:00pm, indoors.
- ❑ Admission: Varies – See website or call

❑   Miscellaneous: Send away for free brochure (or call): P.O. Box
       546, Bardstown, KY 40004. The shows last over 2 hours. You
       may want to consider your child's attention span - especially late
       evening.

Performed under the stars for a romantic setting, this is a good
follow up to your tour of My Old Kentucky Home up on the
hill above the theatre. Spectacular period costumes, lively music,
dances and more than 50 toe-stomping Foster songs including
"Camptown Races" and "Oh, Susanna" - everyone knows them.
Did you know Foster was America's first great composer?

TRIMBLE COUNTY OLD STONE JAIL & COUNTY COURTHOUSE

Court Street

Bedford 40006

❑   Activity: Kentucky History
❑   Phone: (800) 325-4290
❑   Hours: Monday-Friday 9:00am-5:00pm, Sat/Sun Noon -5:00pm.
❑   Admission: FREE

The 1880 courthouse and jail on the courthouse lawn is where
the abolitionist Delia Webster, of the Underground Railroad,
was imprisoned prior to being sent north by horseback. There's a
museum and visitor's center also.

GENERAL BUTLER STATE RESORT PARK

PO Box 325 (I-71 at Carrollton - KY 227)

Carrollton 41008

❑   Activity: Outdoors
❑   Phone: (502) 732-4384 or (800) 325-0078
       Web: www.kystateparks.com

This resort pays tribute to one of Kentucky's foremost military
families, namely General William Orlando Butler. Beginning in

colonial times through the Civil War, the military fame of the Butler family is known well and displayed at the Butler-Turpin Historic House. See the 1859 furnished home full of heirlooms (Tours are February-December, three times daily for $1-3 admission). Also in the park is a hilltop lodge, hiking, tennis, cottages, a campground, a marina, rental boats, a pool and beach, mini-golf and recreation programs.

BERNHEIM FOREST

KY 245 (I-65 exit 112)

Clermont 40110

❑   Activity: Outdoors
❑   Phone: (502) 955-8512, **Web: www.bernheim.org**
❑   Hours: Center, Daily 9am-5pm. Park, 7:00am to sunset. Closed
     Christmas and New Year's.
❑   Admission: Only charged Saturday, Sunday & Holidays. $5.00
     per vehicle.

The official state arboretum with 2000 plants identified, a 14,000 acre forest, 3.5 miles of hiking trails, a fishing lake and visitors center. Take the auto tour of sculpture (we liked "Emerged" and "Lightning" - made from a tree hit by lightning) or stop in the Birds of Prey Building or Live Deer Pen. Get a Scavenger Hunt list before you hit the trails.

FREEMAN LAKE PARK

North US 31 W

Elizabethtown 42701

❑   Activity: Museums
❑   Phone: (800) 437-0092
❑   Hours: Saturday, 10:00am-6pm, Sunday, 1:00-6:00pm (June-
     September)
❑   Admission: Donations

On the campus of this park are three historic homes. The Lincoln Heritage House is a double log house crafted in part by Abraham Lincoln's father. The Sarah Bush Johnston Lincoln Memorial Cabin is a replica of the home of Sarah Bush Johnston's Elizabethtown home at the time she married Thomas Lincoln. Finally, the One Room School House was originally built in Summitt, KY in 1892 and considered the finest school in the county.

HISTORIC DOWNTOWN ELIZABETH WALKING TOUR

Downtown, **Elizabethtown** 42701

- ❑   Activity: Kentucky History
- ❑   Phone: (800) 437-0092
- ❑   Hours: Thursday at 7:00pm (June-August)
- ❑   Admission: FREE

The tour walks along 25 historic sites and buildings. Along the way, historical characters dramatically reveal their part in the town's history (with characters like General Custer). It's a whimsical "meet and greet" and a great way for kids to understand the personalities behind the history.

ROUGH RIVER DAM STATE RESORT PARK

450 Lodge Road (Western Parkway to KY 79 north at Caneyville)

Falls of Rough 40119

- ❑   Activity: Outdoors
- ❑   Phone: (270) 257-2311 and (800) 325-1713
  Web: www.kystateparks.com
- ❑   Miscellaneous: Pine Knob Theatre - musical comedy and folklore, Friday & Saturday nights, June-September. Phone: (270) 879-8190.

Fine fishing waters can be found in the deep waters of Rough River. Fishing or not, there's also boat rentals, a lodge, cottages, dining, a beach, campgrounds, some hiking trails, tennis, golf, mini-golf and recreation programs surrounding the approximately 5000 acre lake. Enjoy the history of the area at old Falls of Rough, a quaint 19th century mill community.

GOLD VAULT - US BULLION DEPOSITORY

(View the Vault from US 31W and Bullion Blvd. On Fort Knox)

Fort Knox 40121

❑   Activity: Tours (Drive-by only)
❑   Phone: (800) 334-7540

Constructed in 1936 at a cost of $560,000 the 2 level vault with door (weighing 20 tons) is guarded 24 hours a day. Made of granite, steel and concrete, it's dimensions are 105 by 121 feet. Gold in the depository is in the form of standard mint bars somewhat smaller than a building brick - each brick weighs about 27.5 pounds. No visitors are allowed (unless you are a United States President or high level cabinet member)…but pictures may be taken of the outside of the building.

PATTON MUSEUM OF CAVALRY & ARMOR

4554 Fayette Avenue

Fort Knox 40121

❑   Activity: Museums
❑   Phone: (800) 334-7540, **Web: www.ltadd.org/radcliff**
❑   Hours: Monday-Friday 9:30am-4:30pm. Saturday-Sunday 10am-4:30pm. Summer weekends and holidays 'til 6:00pm.
❑   Admission: FREE

A museum of military history of armor and cavalry. You'll see General S. Patton's personal belongings, a modified Patton jeep, and a Sherman tank. The highlight for kids is probably the American and Foreign armored vehicles - how they've changed. Most are displayed outside. The largest tank was never used - why? Military (mini) dioramas (with little army men) depict offensive and defensive strategies.

WEST CLINTON
MENNONITE CHURCH

COUNTRY PLACE JAMBOREE

60 Old Sheeppen Road (off US 60 west)

Frankfort 40601

❑   Activity: The Arts
❑   Phone: (502) 223-2359

On any given Saturday night, you'll find a three-hour show that presents the best in traditional country/gospel and bluegrass music or comedy. The concession stand offers home cooking with all the trimmings. A place for the whole family to enjoy and become a "FAMILY AGAIN".

EXECUTIVE MANSION

Capital Avenue building Complex
(next to the Capitol building and overlooking the KY River)

Frankfort 40601

❑   Activity: Kentucky History
❑   Phone: (502) 564-8004
      Web: www.state.ky.us\agencies\gov\mansion.htm
❑   Hours: Tuesday & Thursday 9:00-11:00am. Also guided tours available by reservation.
❑   Admission: FREE

Here, sitting in a beautiful setting, is the official Governor's residence. Modeled after Marie Antionette's summer villa, the rooms you'll see on the tour are the state dining room, ballroom, reception room and formal salon - all rooms designed for "meet and greet" activities.

KENTUCKY HISTORY CENTER

100 West Broadway Street (Downtown)

Frankfort 40601

❑   Activity: Kentucky History
❑   Phone: (502) 564-1792 or (877) 4-HISTORY
      Web: www.kyhistory.org

❏   Hours: Tuesday-Saturday 10:00am-5:00pm, Sunday 1:00-
    5:00pm. Also Thursdays 'til 8:00pm. Closed holiday weekends.
❏   Admission: FREE
❏   Tours: Guided and self-guided.
❏   Miscellaneous: 1792 Museum Store, a world class genealogical
    research library, changing exhibit gallery.

This large museum includes the most expansive part - the permanent interactive exhibit titled " A Kentucky Journey". Explore 10 distinct time periods in KY history - touching all regions, counties and peoples of the state. Hands-on activities and dioramas include voices and music from that time period. Begin with a lifelike repro of the view of the Cumberland Gap. Then, on to: Prehistoric Native Americans hunting in woodlands; Pioneer walk-thru flat boat; Battles of Perryville or the "Houses Divided" in the Civil War; Southern Exposition of 1880 prototypes of very unusual inventions; Simulated Coal Mine; and the Present - George Clooney's scrubs signed by the ER cast, copy of Primetime Live script donated by Diane Sawyer, PapaJohn's Pizza, KFC, Ashland Oil, Corvette and Toyota. There's so much to read and view - all Kentuckians should visit often to learn a little something new each time.

KENTUCKY MILITARY HISTORY MUSEUM

East Main Street at Capital Avenue (Old State Arsenal, US 60)

Frankfort 40601

❏   Activity: Kentucky History
❏   Phone: (877) 4-HISTORY, **Web: www.kyhistory.org**
❏   Hours: Tuesday-Saturday 10:00am-5:00pm, Sunday 1:00-
    5:00pm.
❏   Admission: FREE

Displays here include a collection of firearms, edged weapons, artillery, uniforms, and flags emphasizing Militia, State Guard, and other volunteer organizations from the Revolution through Operation Desert Storm. Mostly geared towards adults or students studying Kentucky's contributions to US Military.

KENTUCKY STATE CAPITOL AREA

Capital Avenue

Frankfort 40601

- ❑ Activity: Kentucky History
- ❑ Phone: (502) 564-3449, **Web: www.state.ky.us**
- ❑ Hours: Monday-Friday 8:00am-4:30pm, Saturday 8:30-4:30pm, Sunday 1:00-4:30pm. Closed major holidays.
- ❑ Admission: FREE
- ❑ Tours: Weekdays, guided and self-guided.
- ❑ Miscellaneous: Gift shop, Snack Bar (homemade entrée for lunch!).

Completed in 1910, the Beaux Arts design features 70 iconic columns, decorative murals (two of Daniel Boone) and sculptures of KY dignitaries. There is a 212 foot high dome with French influences throughout (Napoleon & Marie Antoinette rooms). Notice all the door knobs bear the state seal. The Floral Clock, located on the West Lawn, is planted with 20,000 colorful flowering plants. The face of this clock is 34 inches in diameter. Its unique because it's tilted above the reflecting pool supported by its 100 ton planter. Throw a coin into the fountain of the clock and make a wish (coins donated to children's charities). Oh, by the way, be sure to stop by the Governor's Office and peek in. They'll offer you a "Govern-mint" as a sweet souvenir of you visit.

KENTUCKY STATE UNIVERSITY

East Main Street

Frankfort 40601

- ❑ Activity: Tours
- ❑ Phone: (502) 567-6000, **Web: www.kysu.edu**
- ❑ Hours: Monday-Friday, 8:00am-4:30pm
- ❑ Admission: FREE

KSU is a small, liberal studies university founded in 1886. Visit Jackson Hall with it's art gallery and Center for Excellence for the Study of Kentucky African Americans. The

Blazer Library is open to the public. Most kids will probably gravitate to the Atwood Agricultural Research Facility and it's 166 acre research farm and King Farouk butterfly/moth collection.

KENTUCKY VIETNAM VETERAN'S MEMORIAL

Coffee Tree Road (Off KY 676)

Frankfort 40601

❑   Activity: Kentucky History
❑   Hours: Dawn to dusk
❑   Admission: FREE

Overlooking the city, the names of the Kentuckians who died in Vietnam are etched in granite beneath the giant memorial sundial. The point of the sundial's shadow actually touches the veteran's name on the anniversary of his death...Incredible! Recognized as one of the most original and unusual memorials in the nation, it is truly touching.

LESLIE MORRIS PARK ON FORT HILL

300 Broadway, Old Capitol Annex

Frankfort 40601

❑   Activity: Kentucky History
❑   Phone: (800) 960-7200, **Web: www.kyhistory.org**
❑   Hours: Daylight hours
❑   Admission: FREE
❑   Tours: self guided tours begin at Fort Hill Visitors Center located on the 1st floor of the Annex.
❑   Miscellaneous: No restroom facilities on Fort Hill.

This Civil War site is where local militia held off an attack by Confederate cavalrymen attempting to invade and destroy the capitol of KY. The walls of Fort Boone still stand, as do the earthworks of a second fort know as the New Redoubt. The walking tour points out the 1864 skirmish site too.

LT. GOVERNOR'S MANSION
420 High Street
Frankfort 40601

- ❑ Activity: Kentucky History
- ❑ Phone: (502) 564-3449, **Web: www.state.ky.us**
- ❑ Hours: Tuesday & Thursday 1:30-3:30pm. Guided tours offered by appointment
- ❑ Admission: FREE

This is the oldest official U.S. executive residence still in use. The federal style mansion was home to 33 KY governors from 1798-1914. Now the official residence of the Lt. Governor, the 1st floor is available to tour. Much of the focus of the tour is mention of seven U.S. presidents who visited and why.

OLD STATE CAPITOL
Broadway and Lewis Street
Frankfort 40601

- ❑ Activity: Kentucky History
- ❑ Phone: (502) 564-3016
  Web: www.kyhistory.org/Museums/Old_state_Capitol.htm
- ❑ Hours: Tuesday-Saturday 10:00am-5:00pm; Sunday 1:00-5:00pm. Closed New Years, Easter, Thanksgiving, and Christmastime.
- ❑ Admission: FREE
- ❑ Tours: Guided tours are available by appointment.

This national landmark, operated by the KY Historical Society, was the seat of government from 1830 to 1910. The most interesting part of the structure is the unique, self-supporting staircase held together by pressure of the circular angles. This was the only pro-Union state capitol occupied by the Confederate army during the Civil War and, in 1900, for a time, the place where Kentuckians threatened to fight their own miniature civil war.

REBECCA-RUTH CANDY

112 East Second Street (Downtown & Capital Avenue - near KY River)

Frankfort 40601

- ❑ Activity: Tours
- ❑ Phone: (502) 223-7475 or (800) 444-3766
- ❑ Store Hours: Monday-Saturday 8:30am-5:30pm, Sunday Noon-5:00pm (Year-round)
- ❑ Admission: FREE
- ❑ Tours: Monday-Saturday, 9:30am-4:30pm (Best times are before 1:00pm). (January-October). 10 minutes, guided.

This candy store business was co-founded in 1919 by two schoolteachers, Rebecca and Ruth. They started in their houses making candy over the holidays. Today Ruth Booe's grandson is owner and hands-on operator of this confectionery (you'll probably bump into him). The highlights include free samples, an educational video, antique cooking furnace with hand stirred copper kettles, production areas and "Edna's Table". A 12 foot curved marble slab was purchased by Ruth for $10 in 1917, now it's named after Edna, an employee of 67 years (ate candy 'til the day she died). They make 100 varieties of confections including some unique to Kentucky at 1000 pounds/day. Cute, small-town, casual way to spend a few minutes in a candy factory - what fun!

SALATO WILDLIFE EDUCATION CENTER

#1 Game Farm Road (US 60), Frankfort 40601

- ❑ Activity: Animals & Farms
- ❑ Phone: (800) 858-1549
  Web: www.state.ky.us\agencies\fw\kdfwr.htm
- ❑ Hours: (May-September)Tuesday-Friday 10:00am-5:00pm, Saturday 10:00am-7:00pm, Sunday 1:00-7:00pm. (October-April) Tuesday-Saturday, 10:00am-5:00pm, Sunday 1:00-5:00pm. Park open sunrise to sunset. Closed most holidays. Open Memorial Day, July 4th, and Labor Day.
- ❑ Admission: FREE

❑   Miscellaneous: 132 acre complex with public fishing, picnicking and wildlife viewing. Kentucky Afield Gift Shop.

This educational center has interactive and interpretive exhibits featuring native KY plants and animals. Wonderfully run by the Department of Wildlife and Fishing, they keep it simple but naturally modern. Begin your viewing with stories told by a Native American girl in the mural called Kentuckians Before Boone. Next, you'll gander at warm water fish like Bass, Bluegill and Catfish. Around the corner view KY Record Fish mounted on a giant board with storyboards that tell cute tales of the "Big Catch". Just around the bend is the most unique site - have you ever seen a live Alligator Snapping Turtle? It was amazing to watch this prehistoric creature perform for us - the combination of claws, scales and turtle shell will catch your attention for sure! Outdoors in several different, easily accessible areas, take a look at live American Bald Eagles, white-tailed deer with wild turkeys, bison and elk or the new bobcat exhibit. Further out on the trail is Dragonfly Marsh observation wetland. What can you find?

VEST-LINDSEY HOUSE
401 Wapping Street, Frankfort 40601

❑   Activity: Museums
❑   Phone: (502) 564-6980, Web: www.frankfortky.org
❑   Hours: Monday-Friday 9:00am-4:00pm.
❑   Admission: FREE
❑   Miscellaneous: State Meeting House for government agencies. You might catch VIP's floating around.

The early 19th century Federal House was the boyhood home of US Senator George Graham Vest. He was a famous trial lawyer, mostly remembered for his famous "Tribute to the Dog" speech, from which is coined the phrase "dog is man's best friend". He was defending a man who's dog had killed a neighbor's sheep. Of special interest to kids is the floor cloth in the dining areas (vs. carpet). It was the forerunner of linoleum. Also, kids can help demo the dumb-waiter used to serve from the downstairs kitchen. Be sure to pick up a copy of Vest's famous speech before you leave.

OLD FORT HARROD STATE PARK

South College Street (US 68, SW of Lexington, near US 127 south)

Harrodsburg 40330

- ☐ Activity: Kentucky History
- ☐ Phone: (859) 734-3314, **Web: www.kystateparks.com**
- ☐ Hours: Fort: 8:30am-5:00pm, Daily (mid-March - October). 8:00am-4:30pm (November-early March). Closed Sunday in January. Open 'til Legend of Daniel Boone show begins, summer. Tuesday-Saturday. Museum: 9:00am-5:30pm (mid-March - November)
- ☐ Admission: $1.00-$3.50 per person.
- ☐ Miscellaneous: Gift Shop, picnicking, animal corral (some petting).

In 1774, Captain James Harrod established the first permanent settlement west of the Alleghenies in the hills of what would become central Kentucky. The reconstructed fort was built near the original. Costumed craftspeople perform pioneer tasks such as broom-making, wood-working, basketry, waving, farming, gardening, blacksmithing and woodworking. The folks even sell their wares in their shops/homes - purchase one as a souvenir. Interact by trying to do some pioneer chores (like dyeing yarn or cooking stew). The most unique spot has to be the frontier schoolhouse. With dirt floors and a pretty schoolteacher you'll learn to use a "hornbook". This is a school slate made of wood with a "laminate" surface made from cow horn chips. The teacher writes the lesson using charcoal and each child holds their "book" in front of them to recite their lessons. And your kids think they have it rough!

LEGEND OF DANIEL BOONE

West Lexington Street (Fort Harrod State Park, outdoors behind the
park in Amphitheater)

Harrodsburg 40330

- ❑ Activity: The Arts
- ❑ Phone: (800) 85-BOONE, **Web: www.boonedrama.com**
- ❑ Hours: (June 15-end of August) Tuesday-Saturday, Showtime is
  8:30pm, Sunday 7:00pm. Approx. 2 hour show with intermission.
- ❑ Admission: $14.00 adults, $12.00 seniors, $8.00 children (12 and
  under). Sunday tickets are $8.00 for everyone.
- ❑ Miscellaneous: Your ticket includes admission to Old Fort
  Harrod State Park (valid after 5:00pm, same day as performance)
  except Sundays. The amphitheatre is set with chairs (not benches)
  as seats.

As the kids adorn their new coon-skin hat, learn the "inside story" of Daniel Boone's dreams and disappointments - get inside his head - what drove him? A storyteller shares with you Kentucky's Frontier Adventure - a professionally acted outdoor drama. It definitely relives the action-packed danger and romance of Boone's exploration and settlement of a new land through the Cumberland Gap. Explosions of excitement burst on stage as you sense the dynamics between the inticement of lush land and game versus the sacred hunting ground of the Shawnee Indians. This land "Kanta-Ke" they planned to protect from all intruders. The play ends with the fiery defense of the fort against a full-scale Indian attack. Everyone concluded that this is truly the best way to learn frontiersmen's amazing challenges. The best way to appreciate a hero's life! You even get to meet and greet the actors afterwards - have them sign your program or Boone cap.

ABRAHAM LINCOLN BIRTHPLACE NATIONAL HISTORIC SITE

2995 Lincoln Farm Road (US 31E south at KY 61)

Hodgenville 42748

- ❑ Activity: Kentucky History
- ❑ Phone: (270) 358-3137, **Web: www.nps.gov/abli**
- ❑ Hours: Memorial Day-Labor Day 10:00am-6:45pm. Rest of year 8:00am-4:45pm. Closed Thanksgiving, Christmas & New Years.
- ❑ Admission: Donations.
- ❑ Picnicking, Hiking. A boardwalk ramp trail is available for strollers and wheelchairs. Near the steps is Sinking Spring used by the family and the 400 year old "boundary" oak tree.

A granite memorial with 56 steps, 30 foot wide, leading to the shrine (the steps signify the number of years of Lincoln's life). Enclosed inside is a log cabin which is the symbolic birthplace of Abraham Lincoln (1809-1865). The Visitor Center houses exhibits on the Lincoln family and a video program on Lincoln's boyhood (humbly produced, as Mr. Lincoln would have wanted it). Our family's highlight was seeing the actual Lincoln family Bible (with study notes written by Lincoln family members)!

LINCOLN JAMBOREE

2579 Lincoln Farm Road

Hodgenville 42748

- ❑ Activity: The Arts
- ❑ Phone: (270) 358-3545
- ❑ Hours: Every Saturday night at 8:30pm.
- ❑ Admission

A well-known country music showplace with family shows since 1954. Country restaurant on premises.

LINCOLN'S BOYHOOD HOME

Knob Creek Farm (US 31E northeast)

Hodgenville 42748

- ❏ Activity: Kentucky History
- ❏ Phone: (502) 549-3741
- ❏ Hours: Summers 10am-6pm. Fall/Spring 10am-5pm. Daily April-October.
- ❏ Admission: up to $1.00 per person.

"**M**y earliest recollection is of the Knob Creek Place" says Mr. Lincoln. Abraham (at two years old) and his parents and sister Sarah lived here from 1811-1816. Here he learned to talk and later recalled memories of childhood here: a field to pick berries; the baby brother who was born and died here; staying by his mother's side and watching her face while listening to her read her bible; short periods of subscription school (he called it "blab" school because you recited lessons all day long); and falling in the swollen Knob Creek while playing on a footlog. It was here where a young boy Lincoln first saw slaves transported along the road in front of his home. You can take a look inside the cabin and read the giant storyboard. You can also call ahead for a guided tour (school groups get a great study bag to use for further study back home). You'll surely appreciate Abraham's poor beginnings - yet be inspired by the accomplishments of a man who didn't come from affluent means.

LINCOLN MUSEUM

66 Lincoln Square

Hodgenville 42748

- ❏ Activity: Museums
- ❏ Phone: (270) 358-3163, **Web: www.lincolnmuseumky.org**
- ❏ Hours: Monday-Saturday 8:30am-5:00pm.
  Sunday 12:30-5:00pm.
- ❏ Admission: $3.00 adults, $2.50 seniors (60+), $1.50 children (5-12).

This two-story museum houses 12 wax figure authentic scenes of great significance in Lincoln's life and our nation's history. The first scene is titled "The Cabin Years" (from local boyhood home) and the last scene #12 is "Ford's Theatre". The 18 minute film shown upstairs is another way to see Lincoln's phases of life. Unlike most wax museums, this one is well lit, not frightening to the younger kids. The scenes are enlightened by the descriptions in the brochure you receive upon paid admission. Well done!

OLDHAM COUNTY HISTORY CENTER

106 North Second Avenue

La Grange 40031

- ❑ Activity: Kentucky History
- ❑ Phone: (502) 222-0826
- ❑ Hours: Tuesday, Wednesday, Friday Noon-5:00pm, Thursday Noon-8:00pm, Saturday 10:00am-5:00pm.
- ❑ Admission: $4.00 adults, $3.00 seniors and students (6-18)

The county has put together a facility with changing exhibits and programs that chronicle the development and history of the area. There's also an outdoor sculpture.

JEFFERSON MEMORIAL FOREST

11311 Mitchell Hill Road

Louisville 40118

- ❑ Activity: Outdoors
- ❑ Phone: (502) 368-5404
- ❑ Hours: Dawn to dusk
- ❑ Admission: FREE

The forest is a woodland tribute to the area citizens who served in the nation's wars. Dedicated as a National Audubon Wildlife Sanctuary, the land has over 5000 acres of forest with streams, birds and wildlife, steep slopes of second growth woods of pine, oak and chestnut. Recreation areas, nature trails and a welcome center.

BELLE OF LOUISVILLE & SPIRIT OF JEFFERSON

401 West River Road (Fourth Street Wharf. I-64 west to Third St. exit,
left onto River Rd., right at Second St.)

Louisville 40202

❑   Activity: Tours

❑   Phone: (502) 574-2355, **Web: www.belleoflouisville.org**

❑   Admission: $10.00 adults, $9.00 seniors (60+), $6.00 children (3-12)

❑   Tours: Belle Sightseeing Cruise, (May 7-Labor Day). Board at
Noon and cruise from 1:00-3:00pm, Tuesday-Sunday. Spirit of
Jefferson kid-friendly, historical cruises include the McAlpine
Locks every 1ˢᵗ Monday of summer months (constructed early
1960's, is over 8600 ft. long and has 9 gates, 22 ft. by 100ft.- best
way to see is by boat) and the Riverside Cruise every weekend in
summer plus Saturdays in Sept. and Oct. (includes tour of historic
Farnsley-Moremen home).

❑   Miscellaneous: Spirit of Jefferson is charming with more modern
updates and usually is used for special cruises. Both boats have
concessions, gift shops and restrooms.

The World's Greatest Steamboat was built in 1914 as the "Idlewild" hauling cargo and people on the Mississippi River. In the mid-1940's she was renamed "Avalon" and began "tramping" (steamboats traveling from one town to another for business transport and shows). As the Avalon, she became the most widely traveled steamer in US history. It is now a National Landmark. Almost 200 feet long and 46 feet wide, she is powered by two steam engines (one port, one starboard) and has three decks with the capacity to carry 800 people. The steam calliope, powered by steam from the engine room, has 32 whistles and a sweet Showboat sound. Be sure to check out the original photos of personnel and similar vessels. While you walking thru the gallery, you'll also be able to chat with the captain and shipmates. Your cruise may be narrated by Captain Mary Miller (an actress portraying the 1ˢᵗ woman captain of a steamboat). You'll hear talk of the olden days and special points of interest like the Falls of the

Ohio fossil bed, Muhammad Ali center, and famous bridges and shipyards. Unique to this historical sightseeing tour was the impressive tie in of a historical steamboat character sharing stories - we'd not seen that before! Also, the captain and engineers and 1st mates were very accessible and happy to sit and spend time answering questions. *NOTE: The narration is key to a good tour. If you can't hear, move closer to a speaker.*

JOE & MIKE'S PRETTY GOOD TOURS

(depart from local hotels)

Louisville 40202

- ❑ Activity: Tours
- ❑ Phone: (502) 459-1247
- ❑ Admission: $20.00 adults, $10.00 children (5-10).
- ❑ Tours: Tours depart major area hotels twice daily. Closed New Years, Easter, Thanksgiving and Christmas.

These bus tours visit the downtown area, the Falls of the Ohio, Churchill Downs and the historic neighborhoods of Old Louisville.

LITTLE LOOM HOUSE

328 Kenwood Hill Road

Louisville 40202

- ❑ Activity: Tours
- ❑ Phone: 502-367-4792
- ❑ Hours: Tuesday-Thursday 9:30am-3:30pm. Closed Thanksgiving and Christmas-New Years.
- ❑ Admission: $3.00 (ages 2+)

Tours, demonstrations, classes on spinning and weaving to persons of all ages. They are devoted to keeping the art of hand-weaving and its history alive. The Loom House is housed in three century-old cabins. A gift shop is on the premises.

LOUISVILLE BALLET

315 East Main Street (performances at the KY Center for the Arts,
5 Riverfront Plaza)

Louisville 40202

- ❑ Activity: The Arts
- ❑ Phone: (502) 583-3150 or 584-7777 tickets
  Web: www.louisvilleballet.org

The State Ballet of KY performs classics like "The Nutcracker",
"Swan Lake" and many children's classics.

LOUISVILLE SCIENCE CENTER

727 West Main Street (Downtown)

Louisville 40202

- ❑ Activity: Museums
- ❑ Phone: (800) 591-2203, **Web: www.louisvillescience.org**
- ❑ Hours: Monday-Saturday 9:30am-5pm (also Friday-Sat. 5-9pm),
  Sunday Noon-6pm; closed Thanksgiving and Christmas.
- ❑ Admission: $6.50 adults, $5.50 seniors (60+) and children (2-12).
  Combo tickets w/ IMAX theatre approx. $2.00 more per person.
- ❑ Miscellaneous: KIDZONE has 45 minute ticket (by request only)
  times every hour except Tuesday and Saturday mornings
  (members only then). IMAX Theatre with many daily showtimes.

As you enter the brightly-colored 40,000 square feet of hands-on science, you might first notice the "Be-in-a-Bubble" or "Bubble Scope" exhibits. Areas covered in the museum include Space Exploration, Egyptian Culture, Natural History and Health. But, our favorite floor has to be the second floor where "The World We Create" and KIDZONE can be found. KIDZONE is for the younger set (age 7 and under) with their adults. Initially, you may sit back and watch the kiddies play with "Stuffee" (giant health toy) or "Splash" (water play) or even "Let's Build" (construction toys, blocks, pulleys and conveyors) areas. However, when you get to "Hop On" or "Take Off" play, the whole family is dressing up and playing pretend. The transportation vehicles are

lifelike, only in a kid-friendly, colorful way. Be a bus, ambulance
or plane driver or passenger using apparatus from real vehicles and
airplanes. A giant "Thumbs Up" to the designers of this giant play
equipment! Youngsters can apply what they learned by tagging
along with older siblings in the "World We Create" (get an Early
Learners Guide from KIDZONE). Now you follow inventions
(many created by Kentuckians) like Building Homes, Reinvent
Your Face, Wind Tunnels, Map Master (find your house),
Toppling Towers or Shake, Rattle and Roll (test structures you
create with blocks). AS they say here – "SCIENTISTS AT
PLAY"!

LOUISVILLE SLUGGER MUSEUM

800 West Main Street (Eighth and Main, downtown. I-64 West or I-65
South, exit Third Street)

Louisville 40202

- ❑   Activity: Tours
- ❑   Phone: (502) 588-7228, **Web: www.slugger.com/museum**
- ❑   Hours: Monday-Saturday 9:00am-5:00pm.
- ❑   Admission $6.00 adults, $5.00 seniors (60+) $3.50 children (6-12)
- ❑   Last Tour begins 1 hour before closing.
- ❑   Miscellaneous: Be sure to take the tour - everyone gets a small
  souvenir bat to take home.

You can't miss the entrance to this place - outside or inside.
The world's largest baseball bat (120 foot, 68 thousand
pounds of steel) rests against the outside wall of the manufacturing
plant and the "lets Play Ball" ball and glove sculpture is the
heaviest such structure. Both are great photo ops. See and touch
the actual bats swung by legendary sluggers like Hank Aaron,
Babe Ruth (thicker at the end), Ty Cobb and Ken Griffey, Jr.
(lighter). Begin with a video called "The Heart of the Game" that
emotionally pays tribute to that magical moment in sports when we
hear the crack of the bat. Now that you're in the mood, go through
an underground locker room and dugout and onto the field. After
the umpire (guide) explains the rules, he shouts "Play Ball" and the

group scatters for pictures, "Chats" with bat boys, and glances at memorabilia from great moments and players. Experience the sensation of a 90 mph pitch coming right at you at the great "Batter Up" famous pitchers display! By the time you've taken another good look at an actual Babe Ruth Home Run bat (see the marks on the bat – each one for a home run!), you'll walk thru a replica Northwest White Ash Forest as you move onto the Hillerich & Bradsby Co. factory. See modern bats made from a round wooden cylinder. They are formed from one pass thru a special lathe and then branded with the Louisville Slugger logo and player's name. This is a great All American place for the whole family!

MUSIC THEATRE LOUISVILLE

624 West Main Street (office) (performances at Iroquois Amphitheater, I-264 to Southern Pkwy, south to New Cut Rd east, right on Kenwood)

Louisville 40202

- ❑ Activity: The Arts
- ❑ Phone: (502) 589-4060 or 361-3100 tickets
  Web: www.artspage.org
- ❑ Hours: Thursday-Saturday 8:30pm, Sunday 7:30pm (late June-August).
- ❑ Admission: Ranges from $12-$18

Professional musicals presented under the stars at Iroquois Park Amphitheater with productions like "Annie".

STAGE ONE

501 West Main Street (performances at the KY Center for the Arts)

Louisville 40202

- ❑ Activity: The Arts
- ❑ Phone: (502) 589-5946
  Web: www.louisvillevisualart.org/firstpage

Their focus is strictly on productions for children and families both at public performances and school outreach programs. Shows like "Huck Finn", "Aladdin", and contemporary Christmas themes like "A Winnie-the-Pooh Christmas" are likely each season.

CAMBERLEY BROWN HOTEL
HOT BROWN

335 West Broadway (Fourth & Broadway, downtown)

Louisville 40202

❑   Activity: Theme Restaurant
❑   Phone: (502) 583-1234

The Kentuckian & Louisville proud open-faced sandwich is worth the visit to the place of origination. Served at lunchtime (mostly), the dish was originally created to save guests the boredom of traditional ham & eggs, usually eaten late in the evening after dinner dances at the hotel. Served on toast, it's an open-faced turkey sandwich with bacon, pimentos and/or tomato slices, and a delicate mornay sauce - served piping hot – yum!. Their lunches are between $6-$12.00. They do have a children's menu (chicken fingers, grilled cheese or PB & J), but you have to ask (around $4.00).

THOMAS EDISON HOUSE

729-31 East Washington Street

Louisville 40202

❑   Activity: Museums
❑   Phone: (502) 585-5247, **Web: www.historichomes.org**
❑   Hours: Tuesday-Saturday 10:00am-2:00pm. Closed New Years, Derby Day, July 4, Thanksgiving, and Christmas Eve/Day.
❑   Admission: $4.00 adults, $3.00 seniors (60+), $2.00 children (6-17)

Although you may think - why take the time to visit a place Edison lived at only a brief time? Well, we highly recommend you don't have the same regrets as the boss that fired Thomas Edison - the reason he left Louisville. The guides here will highlight many points of the famous inventors life including working on the railroad, learning Morse Code (try it yourself in his room) to being fired and turning out his first invention, the stock ticker. A great video describes the inventor's life. Did you know he actually started General Electric? Some of his 1093 patents are on display including: early motion pictures (the first one was of a man sneezing!), phonograph, dictating machines, and a collection of electric light bulbs. They have cute light bulb souvenirs to chose from and a picture of our favorite invention - the Power Nap! You have to go just to get the scoop on that!

TOONERVILLE II TROLLEY

Fourth Avenue (Riverfront to Broadway), **Louisville** 40202

- ❑   Activity: Tours
- ❑   Phone: (502) 585-1234
- ❑   Hours: Monday-Friday 7:30am-11:00pm approx. every 12 minutes. Saturday 9:30am-11:00pm every 12 minutes
- ❑   Admission: FREE

The trolley travels from the Galt House to The Camberley Brown Hotel and Theater Square with many other stops along the way in the downtown area.

TOWBOAT ANNIE'S RIVER CAFÉ

201 West River Road (Louisville wharf between 2nd & 3rd Streets)

Louisville 40202

- ❑   Activity: Theme Restaurant
- ❑   Phone: (502) 589-2010
- ❑   Hours: Sunday thru Thursday from 11:00am to 10:00pm. Friday and Saturday from 11:00am to 11:00pm.
- ❑   Admission: Moderate prices serving lunch and dinner. Children's Menu.

Towboat Annie's dropped anchor at the wharf in April of 1997 docked between the Belle of Louisville and the Star of Louisville. She enjoyed a long history as a working riverboat pushing barges for decades. Now converted into a dining boat, the outdoor deck offers open air dining with the sights and sounds of the river traffic, but enclosed air conditioned comfortable dining is available too. Try a Deckhand Burger, Boathouse Club Sandwich or Deck Barge Chocolate Nut Pie.

LOUISVILLE STONEWARE COMPANY
731 Brent Street (I-65 off Broadway Street exit east to
Barret Street, turn right)

Louisville 40204

- ❑ Activity: Tours
- ❑ Phone: (502) 582-1900
  Web: www.louisvillestoneware.com
- ❑ Hours: Monday-Saturday 9:00am-6:00pm
- ❑ Admission: FREE
- ❑ Tours: Monday-Saturday 9am-3pm. Scheduled at 10:30am and 2:30pm. 35-40 minutes long.
- ❑ Miscellaneous: Paint your own pottery workshop - pay by the item - excellent way to end tour (make pre-arrangements with 5 or more).

Nationally famous hand-painted pottery (dinnerware, ovenware, giftware) since 1879. On tour, see the entire process. Begin at the Raw Clay Storage Bin where mounds of dry clay are stacked as tall as your garage. They next mix raw clay with water, take out air bubbles and finally extrude clay fit for the potter's wheel. Unusually shaped pieces (like birdhouses) are cast upstairs. You'll see the jigger production pieces created on a potters wheel with molds and the potter's special trained touch. The handles are all hand formed by two quiet, artistic women. There's a large room full of women painting trains, fish, Noah's Ark, etc. on the wares. You next see the pieces dipped and set to dry in kilns. *Note: We think the best souvenirs of all are those hand-made, especially by your kids. For around $12.00 your kids can create their own design on pottery made here. What a wonderful way to have kids apply what they just saw being made to their own creation!*

AMERICAN PRINTING HOUSE FOR THE BLIND

1839 Frankfort Avenue (I-64 and US 42 east)

Louisville 40206

❏   Activity: Tours
❏   Phone: (800) 223-1839 or (502) 895-2405, **Web: www.aph.org**
❏   Hours: Monday-Friday 8:30am-4:30pm. Closed holidays.
❏   Admission: FREE
❏   Tours: Monday-Thursday at 10:00am and 2:00pm. Make reservations.

Browse through a Braille magazine as you wait for your tour to begin. Founded in 1858, this place is one of the world's largest and oldest printing companies creating products for the visually-impaired. You'll start in the hands-on area (our favorite part - truly fascinating - really!) where visitors can actually learn some of the Braille alphabet, read a popular book in both Braille and written word, or test a talking color analyzer that helps the color-blind match their clothing. Try your math skills with multiplication cards for the blind. Next, briefly tour the plant where they print, bind and proofread all kinds of books and magazines. The museum displays embossed books, early mechanical Braille writers and tactile maps and globes. This is also where you take home a hand-made souvenir of you name typed in Braille. A truly curious, enchanting place! Could you guess what would possibly be their largest Braille project ever? - The World Book Encyclopedia - 145 volumes (see it!).

HADLEY POTTERY

1570 Story Avenue (halfway between Amer. Printing & Edison's Home)

Louisville 40206

❏   Activity: Tours
❏   Phone: (502) 584-2171, **Web:www.hadleypottery.com**

- ❑ Hours: Store hours are M-F from 8:30 a.m. to 5:00 p.m. Eastern time and Saturday from 9:00 a.m. to 1:00 p.m. Saturday hours are extended from the second week in November until Christmas.
- ❑ Admission: FREE
- ❑ Tours: Monday-Friday at 2:00pm (except in the summer when the temp. is over 85 degrees). No age restrictions however small children and elderly or handicapped will not be able to easily manage the very steep staircase to the basement where most of the activity occurs. Some young children feel the basement is also dark and scary.

Pottery by Mary Alice Hadley has an international reputation and is known for it's whimsical designs of clay stoneware. They use a process (you will see during the tour) called "underglaze decoration". The pottery is fired only one time; and this single fire process produces ware with a maximum bond between the body, decoration and glaze, with the result that the decoration is as permanent as the piece. In ware produced by the alternate process of separate firings for the body, glaze and decoration, as is the practice with most dinnerware, the decoration (and sometimes the glaze) is readily subject to abrasion and the chemical action of strong cleaning solutions and to crazing. The high temperature limits the range of colors that can be used in applying decoration. Colors adaptable for use with the white over-glaze are blue, green and rust, with blue-black and yellow available under special circumstances. You'll see artisans hand-painting with these colors on the second floor. Most children like the painting area best.

JOSEPH A. CALLOWAY ARCHEOLOGICAL MUSEUM

2825 Lexington Road (Southern Baptist Theological Seminary)

Louisville 40206

- ❑ Activity: Museums
- ❑ Phone: (502) 897-4141
- ❑ Hours: Monday-Friday, 8:00am-4:30pm

B illy Graham's archives, a copy of the Rosetta Stone and a
2,700 year-old mummy are featured in this collection of
ancient Near Eastern and Egyptian artifacts.

LOCUST GROVE HISTORIC HOME

561 Blankenbaker Lane (I-264 exit 22, US 42 west or
I-71 exit 2, follow signs)

Louisville 40207

- ❑   Activity: Kentucky History
- ❑   Phone: (502) 897-9845, **Web: www.locustgrove.org**
- ❑   Hours: Monday-Saturday 10:00am-4:30pm, Sunday 1:30-
       4:30pm. Hands-on History open Tuesday-Saturday 11:00am-
       3:00pm, June-August. Closed New Years, Easter, Derby Day,
       Thanksgiving, and Christmas.
- ❑   Admission: $4.00 adults, $3.00 seniors (60+), $2.00 children (6-
       12). $2.00 extra per child for Hands-on History.
- ❑   Tours: Monday-Saturday at 10:15, 11:15am, 12:15pm, 1:30pm,
       2:30pm and 3:30pm.
- ❑   Miscellaneous: Pioneer Days or Woodworking Camp available in
       summer. Gift Shop. Video about history of site shown in visitor's
       center.

T he retirement home (beginning in 1809) of George Rogers
Clark - a frontiersman and Revolutionary War General. The
mansion, garden and nine outbuildings are furnished in period.
Start in the parlor room where such guests as Presidents James
Monroe, Zachary Taylor or Andrew Jackson were greeted. Also
Lewis & Clark (William) visited and stored artifacts from
exhibitions in the ballroom upstairs. In the Dining Room you'll
find out why sugar was kept in large cabinets under lock & key.
Why was the letter "J" missing from the alphabet in pioneer days?
Did you know settlers (pre Civil War) wore shoes with no left or
right foot distinction? The Hands-On History Cabin is highly
recommended (summer only). This log cabin is where children can

try on clothing reproductions and sort through the contents of a Revolutionary War soldier's trunk. Kids can also try quilting, weaving, pioneer games, carding wool, surveying and mapping a new city or writing with a real quill pen. Photos in this area make wonderful souvenirs - great learning too.

KENTUCKY DERBY MUSEUM AND CHURCHILL DOWNS

704 Central Avenue (I-264 & Taylor Blvd., Follow signs)

Louisville 40208

- ❑ Activity: Museums
- ❑ Phone: (502) 637-1111, **www.derbymuseum.org**
- ❑ Hours: Monday-Saturday 9:00am-5:00pm, Sunday, Noon-5:00pm. Closed Oaks and Derby days (first Friday/Sat. in May), Thanksgiving and Christmas.
- ❑ Admission: $7.00 adults, $6.00 seniors (55+), $3.00 (5-12)
- ❑ Miscellaneous: Finish Line Shop, Derby Café(lunch). Half hour walking tour of Churchill Downs (weather permitting).

Although the actual Derby Day and Churchill Downs races may not be appropriate for the young kids, the Museum and Tour of Churchill Downs is fun for the family. The museum has 3 floors of displays that showcase thoroughbred racing in the Derby - the greatest two minutes in sports. Different areas focus on: The Horses (owners and trainers, too), The Jockeys and Derby Day. The 360 degree audiovisual recreation is a must see. Located in the center of the first floor, the circular theatre really captures the "feeling" of all people involved. Other highlights are the Starting Gate (you walk thru one as you enter the museum); "Weigh in Please" exhibit where you weigh yourself the day of the race and compare your weight to an average jockey (they average 126 pounds). Finally, our favorite, "Riders Up" - try riding like a jockey on a horse in position to win the race. Don't sit down on the saddle - you'll lose the race!

SPEED ART MUSEUM

2035 South Third Street (exit I-65 to St. Catherine, Arthur St. or
Eastern Parkway - adjacent to the Univ. of Louisville)

Louisville 40208

❑   Activity: The Arts
❑   Phone: (502) 634-2700, **Web: www.speedmuseum.org**
❑   Hours: Tuesday, Wednesday & Friday 10:30am-4:00pm.
      Thursday, 10:30am-8:00pm. Saturday, 10:30am-5:00pm and
      Sunday, Noon-5:00pm.
❑   Admission: $3.50 ages 2+ to Art Sparks. Admission to the
      Speed's Permanent Collection is free.
❑   Miscellaneous: Café Bristol open for lunch Tuesday-Saturday.
      Gift shop.

Although a planned group tour of any significant art museum is a wonderful cultural experience for children, the Art Sparks Interactive Gallery inside this museum makes this art museum the best for kids. Don a Dutch collar and cape and play Rembrandt, dance inside a video artwork, build scale models of downtown skylines, or turn your picture into pop art. In the Electronic Art Room, young visitors can create digital art while visiting museums around the world via the Internet. If you venture, as a family, into the "grown-up" galleries be sure to get a Gallery Pack, a kid-size bag filled with puzzles, seek-and-find, and other hand-outs that take "boring" out of the kid's vocabulary.

PORTLAND MUSEUM

2308 Portland Avenue

Louisville 40212

❑   Activity: Museums
❑   Phone: (506) 776-7678
❑   Hours: Weekdays 10:00am-4:30pm
❑   Admission: $2.00 adults, $1.50 seniors and students. Wednesday
      is "donation day" with FREE admission.

Do newsreels of the 1937 flood or a terrain model of the Falls of the Ohio fossil bed interest you? Study 19th century times (when the town was a thriving river port) through dioramas and mannequins titled "Portland: the Land, the River and the People". The museum is housed in Beech Grove, built in 1852 as a country estate. It also features a 23 minute historical light & sound show.

LOUISVILLE ZOO

1100 Trevilian Way (I-264 exit 14), **Louisville 40213**

- ❑ Activity: Animals & Farms
- ❑ Phone: (502) 459-2181, **Web: www.louisvillezoo.org**
- ❑ Hours: Daily, 10:00am-5:00pm (April-Labor Day); only open 'til 4:00pm rest of year. Closed New Years, Thanksgiving and Christmas. Last entrance is one hour before closing.
- ❑ Admission: $7.95 adults, $5.95 seniors (60+), $4.95 children (3-11)
- ❑ Miscellaneous: Mini-train ride circling zoo. Picnicking spots.

The Mammal and bird exhibits here are arranged by geographic regions. One of the largest arachnid (spiders, centipedes) exhibits is here and it's the only one like it in the U.S. The Islands Pavilion, Indonesian Village is home to tigers and orangutans; there's a walk-thru aviary; the Aquarium has a rainforest, reptiles and fish; the petting zoo features African farm animals; and the MetaZoo Education Center provides amphibian exhibits and microscopes through which small creatures can be viewed.

S.A.R. HISTORICAL MUSEUM

1000 South Fourth Street

Louisville 40216

- ❑ Activity: Museums
- ❑ Phone: (502) 589-1776,
- ❑ Hours: Monday-Friday, 9:30am-4:30pm
- ❑ Admission: FREE

The national headquarters of the Sons of the American Revolution Historical Museum features a continuing program of acquisitions for display, ranging from objects related to the U.S. as it emerged as a new nation to artifacts of the Revolutionary War and Early American decorative arts. Look for the flag from the War of 1812.

LOUISVILLE MOTOR SPEEDWAY

1900 Outer Loop (I-75 exit 127)

Louisville 40219

- ❑   Activity: Sports
- ❑   Phone: (502) 966-2277
- ❑   Hours: Friday & Saturday at around 7:00pm (April-September)
- ❑   Admission charged

The speedway features NASCAR sanctioned racing on a 3/8 mile asphalt oval track with a figure-8 design.

HAWKS VIEW GLASS BLOWING GALLERY

170 Carter Avenue (I-65 exit 121 E to Bluelick Road N to Carter Ave.)

Louisville 40229

- ❑   Activity: Tours
- ❑   Phone: (502) 955-1010, **Web: www.hawksview.com**
- ❑   Hours: Monday-Saturday 10:00am-5:00pm.
- ❑   Admission: FREE
- ❑   Tours: Daily, groups must have appointments. Best to call ahead for best viewing times each week.

Tour this facility and watch artists create small and large unusually shaped glass blown art. Although the thought of gift glass art may not appeal to parents with young children (to display in their home), the idea of purchases as gifts will certainly appeal to you more after watching something being created. Try to figure out which shape they're forming before they finish (there's a good chance it may be something with fins or feathers).

LOUISVILLE RIVER BATS

401 East Main Street (Louisville Slugger Field)

Louisville 40233

- ❑ Activity: Sports
- ❑ Phone: (502) 367-9121, **Web: www.batsbaseball.com**
- ❑ Season: April-September
- ❑ Admission charged

AAA professional baseball farm club for the Cincinnati Reds.

E.P. TOM SAWYER STATE PARK

3000 Freys Hill Road (Gene Snyder Freeway northeast to westbound Westport Road exit)

Louisville 40241

- ❑ Activity: Outdoors
- ❑ Phone: (502) 426-8950, **Web: www.kystateparks.com**

B est known for the following unique amenities: an archery park, a radio controlled airfield, a summer aquatics program, the bicycle moto-cross track or indoor team sports in the park's gymnasium. There's also a few miles of hiking trails.

SIX FLAGS KENTUCKY KINGDOM

(I-65 & 1-264), 937 Phillips Lane, KY Fair Expo Center

Louisville 40241

- ❑ Activity: Amusements
- ❑ Phone: (502) 366-2231
  Web: www.sixflags.com/kentucky kingdom
- ❑ Hours: Open daily June-August beginning at 10:00am or
  11:00am til dark; Weekends only in April, May, September and
  October. Hours vary during the Kentucky State Fair from mid-
  to-late August. Hurricane Bay open daily 11:00am-7:00pm,
  Memorial Day - late September (weather permitting).

❑   Admission: General approx. $30.00. Seniors (over 54) and kids
      under 48 inches tall are approx. half price. Additional fee for
      dragsters and during the Kentucky State Fair. Parking $3.00.

Young ones will love the Looney Tunes character shows, the sing-along musical shows and the special areas with kiddie rides. The older children will gravitate towards the virtual reality ride, a 16-story free-fall ride, and the world's longest stand-up coaster (plus 6 other coasters!). The whole family will have fun at Hurricane Bay waterpark (included in admission). With a 750,000 gallon wave pool, giant waterslides, water tubing and kiddie areas – this is a great way to cool off. There's also a newer family roller coaster where every ride car is individual so you always feel like the "lead" car (this coaster is not as steep and a great way to "graduate" from the kiddie rides). Food, games and traditional rides are offered throughout the park and changing areas are available in Hurricane Bay.

BUCKLEY WILDLIFE SANCTUARY

1035 Germany Road (I-64 exit 58, US 60 east, KY 1681, 1650 & 1964)

Millville 40601

❑   Activity: Animals & Farms
❑   Phone: (859) 873-5711
❑   Hours: Wednesday-Friday 9:00am-5:00pm, Saturday & Sunday
      9:00am-6:00pm. Closed holidays. Nature Center Building & Gift
      shop open weekends only 1:00-6:00pm and for special programs.
      Closed Jan. & Feb.
❑   Admission: $2.00adults, $1.00 children. Price for special events
      vary.

Observe wildlife at the bird blind, hiking trails, fields, forests and wet areas. The trails meander along the KY River, bluegrass and havens for birds, mammals and wildflowers.

KENTUCKY RAILWAY MUSEUM

136 South Main Street (BG Parkway exit 10; KY 52 or US 31E
between Bardstown & Hodgenville), **New Haven** 40051

- ❑ Activity: Museums
- ❑ Phone: (800) 272-0152 or (502) 549-5470
  Web: www.kyrail.org
- ❑ Hours: Museum: Monday-Saturday 10am-4pm, Sunday 1-4pm
  (March-December). Rail Ride: Weekends (March-May and
  October-mid December). Tuesday-Sunday (May-September).
  Departures at 11am & 2pm - Boston Depot. Departures at 1pm &
  3:30pm - New Haven Depot.
- ❑ Admission: Museum only: $3.00 adult, $1.00 child (3-12). Train
  ticket (includes museum): $12.50 adult, $8.00 child (3-12).
  Higher fares for Steam Weekends & Locomotive Cab Rides (ride
  with the engineers).
- ❑ Museum Gift Shop with lots of railroad-themed items. See
  seasonal & Special Events chapter for events including train
  robberies and special holiday train rides. Call ahead to see if
  "Thomas the Tank Engine" is visiting this year!

Ride through a scenic and historic Rolling Fork River Valley.
Pass woodlands, farmlands and small communities. Learn
about the engine and coaches you are riding on. The 22 mile, 1 ½
hour journey is powered by steam or diesel locomotive carrying
authentic coaches on the rails. The museum houses a collection of
artifacts and memorabilia in a replica of the original New Haven
depot. The kids love the sleeping car exhibit, serving cart, railway
post office and track bicycle inspection car. You can also watch
several different toy train layouts operate in the model train center.
Also see some layouts under construction. The train ride is smooth -
parents could bring a magazine and the kids maybe an activity book.
A Railway Coloring Book (given to each child on the trip back) is a
fun souvenir (be sure to bring your own crayons).

HENRY'S ARK

7801 Rose Island Road (the farm borders the Ohio River - 10 miles from Louisville)

Prospect 40059

- ❑   Activity: Animals & Farms
- ❑   Phone: (502) 228-0746
- ❑   Hours: Tuesday-Sunday daylight hours (9:00am-sunset)
- ❑   Admission: FREE. $1.00 donation encouraged.

A privately owned unique petting zoo situated on a 600+ acre horse and cattle farm.   Unique because most of it's inhabitants are touchable.   Tour the outback by trolley and get close-up to larger animals like bison, elk, yak and watusi cattle and smaller animals like ponies, donkeys, sheep and goats. Visitors are encouraged to bring carrots, celery and soda crackers to hand feed the animals. The Ark also furnishes alfalfa cubes for trolley passengers to hand feed bison and elk. The closest you'll ever get to playing "Zookeeper" without extensive training!

BUFFALO CROSSING

1140 Bagdad Road, (Highway 12)

Shelbyville 40065

- ❑   Activity: Animals & Farms
- ❑   Phone:(502) 647-1792, **Web: www.bluegrassbison.com**
- ❑   Hours: Tuesday-Sunday 11:00am-9:00pm.

B uffalo Crossing is located on BlueGrass Bison, a 1,000-acre, working buffalo ranch. Visitors to Buffalo Crossing can catch a glimpse of live buffalo (look for the largest, Chief Joseph) grazing in their natural habitat, as well as visit a unique petting zoo featuring small frontier animals and large exotic animals alike. Restaurant available.

LINCOLN HOMESTEAD STATE PARK

5079 Lincoln Park Road (BG Parkway to US 150 east or KY 555 south.
On KY 528 and 438)

Springfield 40069

- ❑   Activity: Kentucky History
- ❑   Phone: (859) 336-7461, **Web: www.kystateparks.com**
- ❑   Hours: Park - dawn to dusk. Museum: May-September, 8:00am-
  6:00pm.
- ❑   Admission to Museum: $1.50 adults, $1.00 children (6-12).
- ❑   Miscellaneous: Gift shop, picnicking.

The Berry Home - Nancy Hanks lived in this home when she was courted by Thomas Lincoln. In the huge living room before the immense fireplace, Thomas proposed to Nancy. A copy of their marriage bond hangs there. In the knolls near the Beech Fork River, the buildings are filled with pioneer furniture. The buildings on site are replicas of the 1782 cabin and blacksmith shop where Lincoln's father was reared and learned his trade. It was also the home of Mordecai Lincoln, a favorite uncle of the President.

TAYLORSVILLE LAKE STATE PARK

PO Box 205 (I-64 exit 32, take KY 55 south to KY 44/KY 248 east)

Taylorsville 40071

- ❑   Activity: Outdoors
- ❑   Phone: (502) 477-8713 or 477-8766 marina
  Web: www.kystateparks.com

This park boasts a new campground perfect for the numerous fishermen or equestrians that love the fishing and horse trails through forested countryside. The Visitor's Center (KY 2239) is a pioneer homestead and the Dam Visitor's Center and Overlook has a theatre and trail to the historic homestead. There's also a marina and boat rentals.

KENTUCKY SPEEDWAY

(I-71 exit 57)

Warsaw 41095

- ❑   Activity: Sports
- ❑   Phone: (888) 652-RACE, **Web: www.kentuckyspeedway.com**

A 1.5 mile tri-oval, state-of-the-art NASCAR track that opened the summer of 2000. Call or visit website for racing schedule.

MUSIC RANCH USA

407 South Street, **West Point** 40177

- ❑   Activity: The Arts
- ❑   Phone: (502) 922-9393, **Web: www.musicranch.com**
- ❑   Hours: Show every Saturday at 7:30pm. Other music shows vary, mostly Friday nights.
- ❑   Admission: under $10.00 adults, ~$3.00 children.
- ❑   Miscellaneous: Chow hall adjacent, open 5:30pm - midnight.

Country jamboree with old time rock, blues, some Bluegrass and gospel.

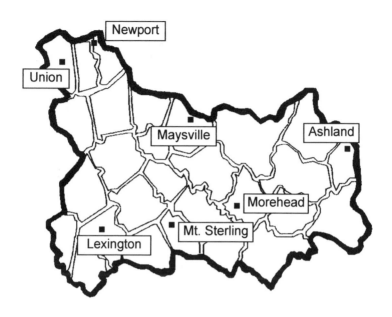

Chapter 2
North East Area

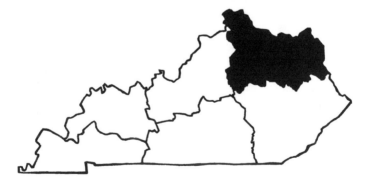

Our Favorites...

- ✓ <u>Kentucky Horse Park</u> – Lexington
- ✓ <u>Lexington Children's Museum</u>
    – Lexington
- ✓ <u>Kentucky Folk Art Center</u>
    – Morehead
- ✓ <u>Minor Clark State Fish Hatchery</u>
    – Morehead
- ✓ <u>Ruth Hunt Candies</u> – Mt. Sterling
- ✓ <u>Newport Aquarium</u> – Newport
- ✓ <u>Big Bone Lick State Park</u> – Union

HIGHLANDS MUSEUM & DISCOVERY CENTER

1620 Winchester Avenue

Ashland 41105

- ☐ Activity: Museums
- ☐ Phone: (606) 329-8888
- ☐ Hours: Tuesday-Saturday 10am-4pm. Closed New Years, July 4, Thanksgiving and Christmastime.
- ☐ Admission: $2.00 adults, $1.00 seniors (60+) and children.

Country music exhibit features the Judds but there's lots more to look at in the Children's Discovery Center. Also see displays on Appalachian culture, Native American artifacts, industrial heritage of the area, antique clothing and a "Granny" Toothman spinner/weaver.

DINSMORE HOMESTEAD

5656 Burlington Pike (I-75/71 exit 181 to KY 18 west)

Burlington

- ☐ Activity: Museums
- ☐ Phone: 859-586-6117, **Web: www.dinsmorefarm.org**
- ☐ Hours: Wednesday, Saturday, Sunday 1:00-5:00pm
- ☐ Admission: $3.00

A Living History Farm with a museum and nature center on the farm of the Dinsmore family who originally came from the deep south. Learn of their benevolent treatment of slaves. Day Camps, Discovery Days or School Living History (hands-on) Tours are your best bet to take advantage of this facility.

BB RIVERBOATS

Covington Landing Docks (I-75 Exit 192)

Covington 41011

❏   Activity: Tours
❏   Phone: (800) 261-8586, **Web: www.bbriverboats.com**
❏   Admission: $10.00+ adults, $9.00+ seniors, $5.00+ children
     (4-12). Prices for meal cruises - generally add $10 or more if
     entertainment.
❏   Tours: 1 ½ hour sightseeing cruises on the Ohio River. Several
     times daily. Reservations required. May-October.

Docked at the foot of Madison Street, see the modern sternwheelers or old-time steamboat. Also theme cruises like mini-vacation, holiday or corporate sponsored. Many cruises offer additional lunch, brunch and dinner cruise options. Sightseeing only cruises offer history of the river plus points of interest on the riverfront.

BEHRINGER / CRAWFORD MUSEUM

1600 Montague Road, Devou Park

Covington 41011

❏   Activity: Museums
❏   Phone: (859) 491-4003
❏   Hours: Tuesday-Friday 10:00am-5:00pm, Saturday-Sunday 1:00-
     5:00pm. Closed holidays.
❏   Admission: $3.00

The museum's collections spans years, embracing Native American Prehistory, Paleontology, Archaeology, the Civil War, and the Underground Railroad.

CARNEGIE VISUAL & PERFORMING ARTS CENTER

1028 Scott Blvd., **Covington** 41011

- ❏ Activity: The Arts
- ❏ Phone: (859) 491-2030

Four art galleries showcase regional artists. Free year 'round arts education programs for youth. The theatre hosts a variety of performance events.

MAINSTRASSE VILLAGE

616 Main Street (I-75 exit 192), **Covington** 41011

- ❏ Activity: The Arts
- ❏ Phone: (800) STAY-NKY, **Web: www.mainstrasse.org**
- ❏ Miscellaneous: Northern KY Visitors Center next to bell tower. Goose Girl bronze sculpture 2 blocks east of tower.

Ongoing restoration and revitalization of a 30 block area in west Covington is now a village with shops and restaurants (try some sweets at the Strudel Shop near the Tower). A favorite with kids is the Carroll Chimes Bell Tower in Goebel Park. The 100 foot bell tower with a 43 bell carillon plays on the hour, from 9:00am-dusk, spring thru Christmas. The bell tower contains one of the 2 American-made animated clocks in the world, with 21 figures performing "The Piped Piper of Hamelin".

RAILWAY MUSEUM OF GREATER CINCINNATI

315 West Southern Avenue, **Covington** 41011

- ❏ Activity: Museums
- ❏ Phone: (859) 491-7245
- ❏ Hours: Saturday-Sunday 12:30-4:30pm (May-October)
- ❏ Admission: $4.00 general

Interiors of railroad cars, railroad memorabilia and locomotives displayed are displayed at this educational museum.

CYTHIANA-HARRISON COUNTY MUSEUM

13 South Walnut Street, Cythiana 41031

- ❑ Activity: Kentucky History
- ❑ Phone: (859) 234-3147 or 5835
  Web: www.cynthianaky.com/museum.html
- ❑ Hours: 10:00am-5:00pm Friday and Saturday
- ❑ Admission: FREE

Focus on military, medical, agricultural and industrial history of the area.

KINCAID LAKE STATE PARK

Rural Route 1, Box 33 (I-275 east to US 27 south to KY 159)

Falmouth 41040

- ❑ Activity: Outdoors
- ❑ Phone: (859) 654-3531, **Web: www.kystateparks.com**

A great big campground with a giant lake make this popular for fishermen, boaters and campers.   Great for watersports, hiking trails, pedal boats, tennis and mini-golf too.

CINCINNATI BENGALS SUMMER TRAINING CAMP

400 East College Street (I-75 and I-64, just 10 miles north of Lexington at the Georgetown College Athletic Complex)

Georgetown 40324

- ❑ Activity: Sports
- ❑ Phone: (502) 863-8009 or 868-6590
  Web: www.bengalscamp.com
- ❑ Hours: Mid-July thru Mid-August.
- ❑ Admission: FREE, fee for parking

Bengals fans can see what the coaches see as the team is forming for the upcoming season of football. FanFest, with activities such as NFL inflatable obstacle course is run during this pre-season camp.

GEORGETOWN / SCOTT COUNTY MUSEUM

229 East Main Street (US 25N)

Georgetown 40324

- ❑ Activity: Kentucky History
- ❑ Phone:(502) 863-2547 or (888) 863-8600
  Web: www.georgetownky.com
- ❑ Hours: Monday-Friday 9:00am-4:00pm
- ❑ Admission: FREE

The carved oak tree wooden sculpture is probably most talked about at this museum housed in the old Post Office building. The museum also has a video to watch, a timeline and several exhibits.

TOYOTA MOTOR MANUFACTURING KENTUCKY

1001 Cherry Blossom Way (I-75 exit 126 east (US 62 E), follow signs to "Visitor's Entrance"

Georgetown 40324

- ❑ Activity: Tours
- ❑ Phone: (800) TMM-4485 or (502) 868-3027
- ❑ Hours: Visitor Center - 9:00am-4:00pm weekdays; to 7:00pm on Thursdays only.
- ❑ Admission: FREE
- ❑ Public Tours: Monday-Friday, 10:00am, Noon, and 2:00pm; with additional 6:00pm tour on Thursday only. Closed major holidays and 3rd week of July. Reservations strongly encouraged. Those without may tour as space permits. Children must be at least 1st graders and accompanied by an adult. School tours are available for grades 4-12.

Can you imagine a building so BIG that it could house <u>over 156 football fields</u> side by side! Wow! When you arrive and begin your tour of Toyota's state-of-the-art North American manufacturing facility, you and your kids will certainly appreciate that you won't have to walk for this tour. Begin your tour at the

Visitor's Center where you get a great taste of what to expect through several interactive exhibits that teach you all about the Toyota JIT (Just in Time) manufacturing philosophy. After viewing a short informational film, you'll board an electric tram (complete with headphones – no loud factory noises here!), to take you on your journey. See steel coils weighing over 34,000 lbs. pressed into body panels and over 700 robots working in precision to create both sedans and mini-vans at this plant. In fact, this is the only manufacturing facility in the world where you will see both vans and cars on the same assembly line at the same time *(how do they do that!)*. Kids will especially love the welding robots that send sparks flying to the factory ceiling (viewed from a safe distance). There are over 4000 welds in each vehicle made. Make sure you tell your kids to watch for the "flying assembly workers" who float in and out of vehicles on specially made chairs (on long booms). The Toyota tire "Yo-Yo" available at the gift shop is a great way to remember this visit!

GREENBO LAKE STATE RESORT PARK

HC 60 Box 562 (I-64 Grayson exit on KY 1 north)

Greenup 41144

❑ Activity: Outdoors
❑ Phone: (606) 473-7324 or (800) 325-0083
   Web: www.kystateparks.com

The name Jesse Stuart (author, educator, Kentucky Poet Laureate and a native of Greenup County)is found throughout these hills at both the lodge and state nature preserve. Read the poet's work in the reading room, swim in the lakeside pool with waterslide, children's wading pool and mist fountains or hike in secluded forests and trails (the Jenny Wiley Trail Heritage Byway). There's also a campground, marina and rental boats, pool, tennis and mini-golf.

UNIVERSITY OF KENTUCKY BASKETBALL MUSEUM

410 Vine Street, Civic Center Shops, 2nd Floor

Lexington 40501

- ❑ Activity: Museums
- ❑ Phone: (800) 269-1953
- ❑ Hours: Wednesday-Saturday 10:00am-5:00pm, Sunday Noon-5:00pm.
- ❑ Admission: $5.00 (ages 6+).

Here they highlight the history of the Nation's most outstanding college basketball programs with lots of video footage of Wildcat play displayed with premium memorabilia. Be sure to look for the ultimate "virtual court" which pits you against some of Kentucky's greatest players or take your picture next to your favorite players action statue.

ASHLAND, THE HENRY CLAY ESTATE

120 Sycamore Road (1.5 miles southeast at the corner of Sycamore Road and Richmond Road - US 25 & KY 922)

Lexington 40502

- ❑ Activity: Museums
- ❑ Phone: (859) 266-8581, **Web: www.henryclay.org**
- ❑ Hours: Monday-Saturday 10:00am-4:30pm, Sunday 1:00-4:30pm.Closed Mondays November-March. Closed January and holidays.
- ❑ Admission: $6.00 adults, $3.00 students, $2.00 children (6-12).
- ❑ Tours: one hour long - guided, given on the hour.
- ❑ Miscellaneous: Food is available in the Outdoors Café open for lunch and snacks. Museum Store.

Henry Clay (1777-1852) was named The Great Compromiser, Harry of the West, Candidate for President and quoted "I'd rather be right than president". Living here most of his adult life, the 18 room mansion is furnished with Clay family possessions. The tour begins with a videotape historical review. On tour, there are also outbuildings on the grounds like the icehouse, smokehouse, dairy cellar, privy/laundry and keepers cottage - all in a park-like setting.

OLD KENTUCKY CANDIES

450 Southland Drive (I-75 exit 115 west to Harrodsburg Rd, right on Lane Allen Road to Southland)

Lexington 40503

- ❏ Activity: Tours
- ❏ Phone: (800) 786-0579, **Web: www.oldkycandy.com**
- ❏ Admission: FREE
- ❏ Tours: Monday-Thursday 9:30am-12:30pm and 1:30-3:00pm. 15 minutes. Best to call ahead for production hours.

Hopefully you'll go on a day when you can watch them make KY Derby Mints or UK molded chocolates. Plenty of samples follow the tour that includes verbal and photo explanations.

MC CONNELL SPRINGS

416 Quarry Drive

Lexington 40504

- ❏ Activity: Outdoors
- ❏ Phone: (859) 225-4073
  Web: www.lfucg.com/Pubinfo/springs.htm

The campsite of the first settlers in the Bluegrass. McConnell Springs is the site where Lexington was founded. It lies within a tract of land claimed by William McConnell in 1775. McConnell Springs has over two miles of trails that wander past historic foundations, stone fences, an old farm pond and lush vegetation. The new Education Center is equipped with a lab with sinks and counter space allowing students to conduct hands-on experiments and textbook research.

PARKETTE DRIVE-IN

1216 E. New Circle Road (between Winchester Road and
Richmond road), **Lexington 40505**

- ❑   Activity: Theme Restaurant
- ❑   Phone: (859) 254-8723
- ❑   Hours: Monday-Thursday 10:00am-10:30pm; Friday & Saturday
  10:00am-11:30pm; Sunday 11:00am-9:00pm.

Very economically priced (combo meals are under $4.00), this place is a step back in time. Since 1951, this "drive-in" ordering eatery is right out of scenes of "Happy Days". After placing your order over the microphone, a delivery girl or boy (adorned in Parkette cap and t-shirt vs. poodle skirt of the 50's) delivers you order windowside. Their menu includes burgers, fried chicken, seafood and the famous "Kentucky Poor Boy" sandwich (double-decker burgers dressed with toppings to the hilt!). Memories meet the pavement when (on Friday nights) the Parkette is host to classic cars and motorcycles. They serve 12,000 customers a week.

UNIVERSITY OF KENTUCKY

South Limestone Street (Visitor Center is at UK Student Center - off
Avenue of Champions -Bounded by Limestone Street, Euclid Ave., and
Rose Street), **Lexington 40506**

- ❑   Activity: Tours
- ❑   Phone: (859) 257-9000
  Web: www.uky.edu (campus guide/map)
- ❑   Admission: FREE
- ❑   Tours: Walking tours are conducted Monday-Friday at 10:00am
  and 2:00pm (also Saturday at 11:00am during the academic year).
  Guided tours of the campus depart from the visitors center in the
  Student Center on Euclid Avenue across from Memorial
  Coliseum.

The 625 acre campus was established in 1865 and enrolls 24,000 students.

University of Kentucky (cont.)

❑   **UK ART MUSEUM** - Singletary Center for the Arts at the
    corner of Euclid and Rose Streets. Changing shows of permanent
    and traveling exhibits. Tours available. Tuesday-Sunday, Noon-
    5:00pm. Closed July 4, Thanksgiving, and Christmas thru New
    Years. (859) 257-5716.

❑   **WEBB MUSEUM OF ANTHROPOLOGY** - Lafferty Hall,
    center of campus. Traces history of humans in Kentucky. Other
    displays highlight the artistry, ingenuity and technology of
    present-day cultures from around the world. Monday-Friday
    8:00am-4:30pm. Closed holidays. (859) 257-7112.

❑   **COLDSTREAM & MAINE CHANCE FARMS** - Newtown
    Park. Used by UK for crop and livestock research. North of
    downtown near I-64/75.

❑   **ARBORETUM PARK** - "A Walk Across Kentucky" showcases
    state vegetation grouped by region. Open dawn to dusk.
    Children's Garden - Alphabet plants and plantings in old tennis
    shoes. Master Gardener - demo Veggie Garden, Fish Pond,
    plants for KY gardens. Be sure to get a colorful map and have
    fun playing the Arboretum Garden Game.

CENTRAL KENTUCKY YOUTH ORCHESTRA
161 North Mill Street (ArtsPlace office)
Lexington 40507

❑   Activity: The Arts
❑   Phone: (859) 254-0796, **Web: www.ckyo.org**

Two orchestras and over 140 talented young people perform
children's concerts. Performed at the Singletary Center or the
Opera House.

KENTUCKY THOROUGHBLADES HOCKEY

410 West Vine Street (Rupp Arena)

Lexington 40507

- ❑ Activity: Sports
- ❑ Phone: (859) 259-1996 tickets or 233-3535 info.
  Web: www.tblades.com
- ❑ Season: October-early April. Games last approx. 3 hours.
- ❑ Admission: $8.00 kids under 12, $10-25 adults
- ❑ Miscellaneous: American Hockey League. Typically families bring kids to games with "family night" or "Free Puck" or "Student Night" themes.

LEXINGTON BALLET

161 North Mill Street (ArtsPlace office)

Lexington 40507

- ❑ Activity: The Arts
- ❑ Phone: (859) 233-3925, **Web: www.lexingtonballet.org**
- ❑ Miscellaneous: Dance training and arts education programs.

With several classic and romantic ballet performances like the Nutcracker and Swan Lake.

LEXINGTON CHILDREN'S MUSEUM

440 West Main Street (Victorian Square, corner of W. Short and Algonquin Streets), Lexington 40507

- ❑ Activity: Museums
- ❑ Phone: (859) 258-3256
  Web: www.lfucg.com/childrensmuseum
- ❑ Hours: Tuesday-Friday 10:00am-6:00pm, Saturday 10:00am-5:00pm, Sunday 1:00-5:00pm. Closed Easter, week after Labor Day, Thanksgiving and Christmas.

- ❑ Admission: $3.00 per person (age 2+). Free parking for up to 3 hours in Victorian Square Garage.
- ❑ Miscellaneous: While you're downtown, stop by Thoroughbred Park on Main Street where 7 life size bronze statues of horses racing are available to climb on for great photo ops!

Hands-on exhibits cover science, nature, history, civics and ecology. Little ones can visit the Toddler Area (under age 3). Everyone will love to make huge bubbles in the Bubble Factory; go Home to world geography and culture; "Walk on the Moon" and even sit in a crater!; create Soil Wars; make a Quake; be a Turtle; Greet the Brainzilla (giant brain that talks to you); Walk thru a Human Heart with many "chamber" rooms; make Me and My Shadow; or play a King Piano. Extremely well done with descriptions that are easy to follow and teach to the children. This is a great family stop and those living in the area should become members so they can attend the interesting monthly workshops. While you're in the Victorian Square area, stop over for soup and sandwich topped off with an old-fashioned soda dessert at Hutchinson's Drug Store. Have fun!

LEXINGTON CHILDREN'S THEATRE

418 West Short Street (downtown)

Lexington 40507

- ❑ Activity: The Arts
- ❑ Phone: (859) 254-9565, **Web: www.lctonstage.org**
- ❑ Admission: $6.50 each or subscription Flex-Tix pricing.

Charlotte's Web, a Christmas Carol, and Rapunzel are examples of the many folklore-based plays offered. Plays are rated for age appropriateness (ex. Age 4+ or Age 9+).

LEXINGTON PHILHARMONIC

161 North Mill Street (ArtsPlace)

Lexington 40507

- ❏ Activity: The Arts
- ❏ Phone: (859) 233-7896 or 233-4226 tickets
   Web: www.lexingtonphilharmonic.org

The Family Series (one-hour musical and visual with activities) and Pops Concerts (Patriotic Concert, Kentucky Christmas Chorus, two free concerts and Picnic with the Pops)

HUNT-MORGAN HOUSE

201 North Mill Street (near 2nd Street, downtown)

Lexington 40508

- ❏ Activity: Museums
- ❏ Phone: (859) 253-0362
- ❏ Admission: $5.00 adults, $3.00 students with ID.
- ❏ Tours: Guided tours Tuesday-Saturday 10:00am-4:00pm, Sunday
   2:00-5:00pm (mid-March to mid-December). Closed
   Thanksgiving. Tours begin ¼ past the hour.

A 1800's Federal-style prominent family home of the Hunt-Morgan families. John Wesley Hunt was the first millionaire of the west (and built this home),   John Hunt Morgan was the "Thunderbolt of the Confederacy" and Thomas Hunt Morgan was the "father of modern genetics" and a Nobel Prize winner.   The architecture of a fan-light doorway and cantilevered staircase mixed with original furnishings and Civil War memorabilia, make this a piece of history based on it's inhabitants.

MARY TODD LINCOLN HOUSE

578 West Main Street

Lexington 40508

- ❑   Activity: Kentucky History
- ❑   Phone: (859) 233-9999
- ❑   Hours: (March 15-November) Tuesday-Saturday 10:00am-
      4:00pm. Closed holidays.
- ❑   Admission: $6.00 adults, $3.00 children (6-12)
- ❑   Tours: Last tour begins 45 minutes before closing. Guided, one
      hour.

The girlhood home of Abraham Lincoln's wife, Mary. The two story, beautiful brick 1803 Georgian-style house is furnished with period furniture from Mary's collection and personal articles of the Lincoln-Todd families. Kids like hearing stories about a famous adults' life as a child. Do you know how many brothers and sisters Mary had (15) or that she had a formal education of 12 years (vs. her husband who really had very little)? Opposites attract.

KENTUCKY HORSE PARK

4089 Iron Works Parkway (I-75 exit 120)

Lexington 40511

- ❑   Activity: Animals & Farms
- ❑   Phone: (800) 678-8813 or (859) 233-4303
      Web: www.kyhorsepark.com
- ❑   Hours: Daily, 9:00am-5:00pm. (March 15-October) Closed on
      Mondays and Tuesdays (November-March 14). Closed
      Thanksgiving, Christmas, and New Years.
- ❑   Admission: $9-12.00 Adults, $5.50-6.50 Children (7-12).
      Children 6 and under free when accompanied by paying adult.
- ❑   Miscellaneous: Clubhouse Restaurant, Campgrounds, Gift Shop,
      Horseback rides ($13+), Pony rides ($13+), Nearly 60 horse
      shows are held here yearly. KY Horse Park framed pictures
      aboard unique breeds ($3). Parking ($2)

D o you have a real horse lover in the family? This is a horse-lover's dream park. It's Kentucky's tribute to one of its famous industries from tiny minis to large draft houses to retired racing stars. Begin with the Visitor Info Center Film - wide screen film "Thou Shalt Fly Without Wings" - depicting man's special relationship with horses both at work and play. Now, go next door to the International Museum of the Horse. Before long, take the horse-drawn trolley tour. Then catch a show at the Hall of Champions - home of retired "equine millionaires" (3x daily). They tell you funny stories about famous horses. Also be sure to catch a show at the Parade of Breeds - show of dozens of breeds of horses with their riders in native costume with music accompaniment (2x daily). Some are used for rugged terrain, pulling, cowboy riding, cavalry, or trailing. Fill the time between shows at the Big Barn (talk with trainers), Draft and Breeds and Carriage Barns, Farrier's and harness maker's shops. The American SaddleHorse Museum - is a multi-image show and exhibit hall located on the premises near the parking lots. (800) 829-4438.

WAVELAND STATE HISTORIC SITE

225 Waveland Museum Lane, 225 Higbee Mill Road (Off US 27 south)

Lexington 40514

- ❑ Activity: Museums
- ❑ Phone: (859) 272-3611, **Web: www.kystateparks.com**
- ❑ Hours: (March-Mid December) Monday-Saturday 10:00am-5:00pm, Sunday 1:00-5:00pm.
- ❑ Admission: $6.00 adults, $5.00 seniors, $3.00 students (age 6+).
- ❑ Tours: On the hour, last tour 4:00pm.
- ❑ Miscellaneous: Picnicking.

T his beautiful 1847 Greek Revival home was built by Joseph Bryan, a grand-nephew of Daniel Boone. Tours focus on the everyday lives of the Bryan Family and the African-Americans who lived and worked there. Included are the icehouse, smokehouse and servants quarters.

RAVEN RUN NATURE SANCTUARY

5888 Jacks Creek Road (off US 25/421 south)

Lexington 40515

- ❑ Activity: Animals & Farms
- ❑ Phone: (859) 272-6105
- ❑ Hours: Daily 9:00am-7:00pm (April-September). 9:00am-5:00pm, rest of year. Trails close 30 minutes before park closing. Closed Thanksgiving and Christmas.
- ❑ Admission: FREE

Follow trails lined with native flora and fauna, rock fences, an historic home, meadow, forest and creeks leading to views of the Kentucky River palisades. The park is also known for the waterfalls and wildflowers. Stop at the nature center too.

AVIATION MUSEUM OF KENTUCKY

4000 Versailles Road (2 miles west of New Circle Rd. on US 60 to Bluegrass Airport Road), Lexington 40544

- ❑ Activity: Museums
- ❑ Phone: (859) 231-1219, **Web: www.aviationky.org**
- ❑ Hours: Tuesday, Thursday, Friday & Saturday 10:00-5:00pm, Sunday 1:00-5:00pm.
- ❑ Admission: $3.00 adults, $2.00 seniors, $1.50 students.

Most interesting to kids is the cockpit you can sit in, the supersonic trainer, and the "Women in Aviation" display. There's also lots of uniforms, model airplanes, actual aircraft (helicopters, a Skyhawk II, and a Quadraplane).

KEENELAND TRACK KITCHEN

4201 Versailles Road (US 60 west)

Lexington 40592

- ❑ Activity: Theme Restaurant
- ❑ Phone: (800) 456-3412, **Web: www.keeneland.com**

❑ Hours: "Breakfast with the Works" buffet served during morning workouts during seasonal race months (usually April and October) daily 6:00am-10:30am. May be Closed Monday, Tuesday and Easter.
❑ Admission: Reasonably priced buffet.

Meet and greet and eat with trainers and jockeys at breakfast during morning workouts.

YATESVILLE LAKE STATE PARK
PO Box 767 (US 23 to Louisa, then west on KY 3)

Louisa 41230

❑ Activity: Outdoors
❑ Phone: (606) 673-1490 or 686-2361 marina
Web: www.kystateparks.com

Full service campsites and marina with rentals are the highlights of this park. The lake and river make for good fishing and along these waters are great scenic overlooks and play areas.

MASON COUNTY MUSEUM
215 Sutton Street

Maysville 41056

❑ Activity: Kentucky History
❑ Phone: (606) 564-5865
❑ Hours: Tuesday-Saturday 10:00am-4:00pm (Jan.-March). Monday-Saturday 10:00am-4:00pm (April-Dec.). Closed holidays.
❑ Admission: small fee

The museum contains two dioramas of the earliest settlement of Maysville, a map collection, a slide show and changing gallery exhibits. Just so you know, this area is one of the largest burley tobacco markets in the world and much of their modern history revolves around this.

MAYSVILLE FLOODWALL MURALS

216 Bridge Street (downtown riverfront)

Maysville 41056

- ❑ Activity: Outdoors
- ❑ Phone: (606) 564-9411
- ❑ Hours: 24 hours a day
- ❑ Admission: FREE

Historical portrayals of the Ohio River by artist Robert Dafford of scouts, nobility who floated down the river, and settlers.

NATIONAL UNDERGROUND RAILROAD MUSEUM

115 East Third Street

Maysville 41056

- ❑ Activity: Museums
- ❑ Phone: (606) 564-6986
  Web: www.coax.net/people/lwf/urmuseum.htm
- ❑ Hours: Monday-Saturday 10:00am-4:00pm
- ❑ Admission: Donations

The museum symbolizes a local effort to preserve and display artifacts that tell the stories of life on the Underground Railroad. The Maysville area is surrounded by freedom stations - crossing the Ohio River north was a preeminent step in escaping bondage.

KENTUCKY FOLK ART CENTER

102 West First Street (I-64 exit 137, follow signs)

Morehead 40351

- ❑ Activity: The Arts
- ❑ Phone: (606) 783-2204, **Web: www.kyfolkart.org**
- ❑ Hours: Monday-Saturday 9:00am-5:00pm (yearlong).
- ❑ Admission: $3.00 (12 and over). $2.00 Seniors.

❑   Miscellaneous: Museum Store with original artworks, Library
    and rotating upstairs Gallery.

Visit the only museum of KY Folk Art, housed in a renovated
    early 1900 grocery warehouse. In the Auditorium, watch a
seven minute video narrated by Rosemary Clooney introducing
visitors to the "World of Wonder" housed within the Center. Look
for recycled material sculpted into George Washington, Dolly
Parton, Uncle Sam and Ronald McDonald. There was a birdhouse
in an old shoe (that's art?). Our favorite was "Precious Memories"
- a monkey made with junk - can you find the cow and chess
piece? From whimsical to religious to political statements are
made through this art.

MINOR CLARK STATE FISH HATCHERY

120 Fish Hatchery Road
(SR 801south (Off I-64), below dam. Farmers/Sharkey exit)

Morehead 40351

❑   Activity: Animals & Farms
❑   Phone: (606) 784-6872
❑   Hours: Monday-Friday 7:00am-3:00pm. Closed holidays.
    Viewing of display pool and ponds anytime.
❑   Admission: FREE

This is among the largest warm water hatcheries in the country
    with 300 acres, 111 ponds, and a few racers (give fish a chance
to exercise). The display pool is wonderful with large and small
largemouth bass, walleye, 2 varieties of striped bass, and muskee to
view up close. Their main objective is to produce fish for Kentucky
waters to enhance opportunities to catch trophy fish.

MOREHEAD STATE UNIVERSITY

University Blvd.

Morehead 40351

❑   Activity: Tours
❑   Phone: (800) 654-1944 or (606) 784-5221

E stablished in 1887, the 500 acre campus enrolls 8300 students and has a history of focusing on Appalachian peoples. The Cora Wilson Stewart Moonlight School building was once used for nighttime reading and writing classes for Appalachian people and an Appalachian Collection is found on the 5th floor of the Camden-Carroll Library Tower. Nearby (KY 377) is the MSU Farm Complex & Arena.

BLUE LICKS BATTLEFIELD STATE RESORT PARK

PO Box 66 (US 68 northeast of Lexington)

Mount Olivet 41064

❑   Activity: Kentucky History
❑   Phone: (659) 289-5507 or (800) 443-7008

I n 1782, Blue Licks was the site of the last Revolutionary War battle in Kentucky. Visit the Pioneer Museum (admission $1.50-$2.00) where you can learn more about the battle plus history of why prehistoric animals, Indians, pioneers and 19th century Southerners came for the salt licks and soothing waters (view a 10 minute video plus tons of relics). The Nature Preserve protects a rare plant - Short's Goldenrod - the only place it's found in the world growing along the rocky buffalo trace. On campus, there's a modern lodge with dining room, cottages, campgrounds, pool, hiking trail, mini-golf and recreation programs.

RUTH HUNT CANDIES

426 West Main Street (new location - 550 North Maysville mid-2001)

Mt. Sterling 40353

- ❑ Activity: Tours
- ❑ Phone: (800) 927-0302, **Web: www.ruthhuntcandy.com**
- ❑ Admission: FREE
- ❑ Tours: Monday-Thursday 10:30am-Noon and 1:00-2:30pm. Best to make appointment in the summer (less production).

"**Y**ou are about to taste a little bit of Kentucky's confectionery history!" In the early 1920s, Ruth Hunt made and served homemade sweets to her bridge club. They were so loved that she decided to open a small candy store in her home, packaging products in coffee tins. On tour, you'll see hot cinnamon suckers being formed on a huge old marble slab, giant copper kettles (how old might they be?), and nuts roasting in the oven. Most of these confections are still made from Ruth's original recipes. Their most famous product is the Blue Monday Sweet Bar - the chocolate covered KY pulled cream candy center, melt-in-your-mouth legend. Let their Blue Monday sweets cure your "Blue Monday". They are also noted as the official assorted candies of Churchill Downs. The treat at the end is to sample a few fresh sweets!

NEWPORT AQUARIUM - OCEANIC ADVENTURES

One Aquarium Way (3rd & York Streets, just over the bridge into Newport. I-71 to I-471 south exit 5 (Rt. 8) to parking garage)

Newport 41011

- ❑ Activity: Animals & Farms
- ❑ Phone: (888) 491-FINS, **Web: www.newportaquarium.com**
- ❑ Hours: Daily 10:00am-7:00pm (Summer), Daily 10am-6pm (Fall/Winter/Spring).
- ❑ Admission: $14.95 adults, $12.95 seniors (65+), $8.95 children (3-12)

❏   Miscellaneous: Lighthouse Café, Gift shop. No strollers past the
    entrance.

As you take the escalator down into the ocean, you'll read thru
a brochure that invites you to explore one million gallons of
water. They use clear, seamless acrylic walls and tunnels that truly
make you want to reach out and touch the fish. Everywhere you
go, remember to look up, look down and keep your ears open - it
truly is a place you have to see with all your senses. 60 different
exhibits take you places you'd probably never go! Rivers of the
World (knifefish); The Bizarre and Beautiful (flashlight fish);
Pirate Theatre (a movie ship - Yo, Ho, Ho!); Shore Gallery (touch
pool where visitors can feel & examine creatures like Mermaid's
Purses or tickle a Horseshoe Crab); Kingdom of Penguins - 16
King Penguins from Japan are set in a winter setting theatre with
video monitor close-ups. Occasionally baby penguins are hatched
and grown in the nursery here! The absolute highlight is the
Surrounded by Sharks exhibit - 85 feet under water! The tunnels
take you thru a shark home - as your child presses his nose against
the acrylic tube - wait - for the first shriek when a shark is sighted
and comes right at you! Don't worry, it's a total thrill that's
completely safe.

WORLD PEACE BELL EXHIBIT CENTER

425 York Street

Newport 41011

❏   Activity: Outdoors
❏   Phone: (859) 261-2526, **Web: www.millenniummonument.com**

The World Peace Bell is the world's largest free swinging bell.
It weighs 66,000 lbs., is 12 feet in diameter and 12 feet high.
Its clapper alone weighs an amazing 6,878 pounds. The yoke in
which it swings weighs an additional 16,512 pounds. This
magnificent bell rings with a powerful, awe-inspiring, deep
resonant tone that is truly a majestic symbol of freedom and peace.
Bell swings and rings each day at noon.

HARRY MILLER LOCK COLLECTION

1014 South Main Street (Lockmasters Inc. training center)

Nicholasville 40356

- ❑ Activity: Museums
- ❑ Phone: (859) 887-9633
- ❑ Hours: Monday, Wednesday and Friday from 1:00-4:00pm.
- ❑ Admission: FREE

See the world's largest lock collection. A brochure details the history of the items showcased. Self-guided tours only.

CARTER CAVES STATE RESORT PARK

344 Caveland Drive (I-64 west to KY 182 north)

Olive Hill 41164

- ❑ Activity: Outdoors
- ❑ Phone: (606) 286-4411 or (800) 325-0059
  Web: www.kystateparks.com

Tour through more than 20 twisting caverns departing from the Welcome Center several times daily ($3.00-5.00). Bat Cave (May-August only) is the protected home of the Social Bat/Indiana Bat. Cascade Cave, with a 30 foot underground waterfall or X Cave with formed luminous stone fans, pipes and spirals are special spots here too. Canoeing down Tygart's Creek (June-August) can be fun or take a guided horseback trail ride. The 20 miles of hiking trails feature such attractions as Box Canyon, Wind Tunnel and Natural Bridge. Property next to this park is Tygart's State Forest with many other trails. Other amenities are a lodge, cottages, campgrounds, a marina with boat rentals, tennis and mini-golf.

GRAYSON LAKE STATE PARK

314 Grayson Lake Park Road (I-64 west to KY 7 south)

Olive Hill 41164

❑   Activity: Outdoors
❑   Phone: (606) 474-9727, **Web: www.kystateparks.com**

Once a favorite campground for Shawnee and Cherokee Indians, this land is full of sheer sandstone canyons and gentle slopes.   Camping is still the favorite here, plus summer musical outdoor drama, a boat launch, and hiking trails.

HOPEWELL MUSEUM

800 Pleasant Street

Paris 40361

❑   Activity: Museums
❑   Phone: (859) 987-7274
❑   Hours: Wednesday-Saturday, Noon-5:00pm,
      Sunday 2:00-4:00pm

Housed in the historic 1909 Beaux Arts-style Paris post office, Hopewell Museum was founded in 1994. The museum features changing exhibits on the art and history of Bourbon County and central Kentucky.

KENTUCKY REPTILE ZOO

1275 Natural Bridge Road
(1 mile south of Mountain Pkwy, exit 33 off KY 11)

Slide 40376

❑   Activity: Animals & Farms
❑   Phone: (606) 663-9160
❑   Hours: Daily Sunday-Thursday 11:00am-6:00pm, Friday-
      Saturday 'til 7:00pm (Memorial Day-Labor Day). Friday-Sunday
      11:00am-6:00pm (March-May, September-November).
❑   Admission: $4.00 adults, $2.50 children (4-15)

The zoo is also a captive born venom lab with extractions and live reptile presentations held daily on the hour from 1:00-5:00pm. The live reptile exhibits include more than 75 species of lizards, turtles, alligators and snakes. The zoo is now breeding successfully to hopefully use the extracted substances to produce medical and research projects. Look for the vide variety of cobras, rattlesnakes and vipers too.

BIG BONE LICK STATE PARK

3380 Beaver Road (I-75 AND KY 338, exit 175, follow signs)

Union 41091

❑   Activity: Outdoors
❑   Phone: (859) 384-3522, **Web: www.kystateparks.com**
❑   Hours: Museum daily summers 8am-8pm. April, May,
      September, October, Monday-Thursday 10am-6pm, Friday-
      Sunday 8am-8pm. Rest of year: Wednesday-Sunday Noon-5pm.
❑   Admission: up to $1.00 per person.
❑   Miscellaneous: Campground, Gift shop, Pool, 2.5 miles of Hiking
      Trails, Tennis, Mini Golf, Picnicking.

The birthplace of American Vertebrate Paleontology. The greatest ice age graveyard ever found! A premier archeological site because great herds of giant mastodons, mammoths, and bison came to the warm salt springs (the springs still bubble today). Some became trapped in the marshy ground and died here, leaving skeletons that have been uncovered from prehistoric times. A walking diorama, the outdoor museum hosts these beasts displayed in their natural habitat. Erosion may still reveal bones (look for them on your hike) especially along the creek. A live buffalo herd now roams the property and your kids can touch Mastodon teeth!

BLUEGRASS SCENIC RAILROAD AND MUSEUM

Woodford County Park (US 62 west)

Versailles 40383

- ❏ Activity: Tours
- ❏ Phone: (859) 873-2476 or (800) 755-2476
  Web: www.bgrm.org
- ❏ Hours: Museum open Saturday 10:00am-3:00pm and Sunday 1:00-3:00pm.
- ❏ Admission:$7.00 adult, $6.00 senior (over 61), $5.00 children (2-12). Museum free.
- ❏ Tours: Departures Saturday at 10:30am, 1:30pm and 3:30pm. Departures Sunday at 1:30pm and 3:30pm. Open Memorial Day weekend thru the third weekend in October plus special seasonal rides listed in another chapter.

R ide on the old Louisville Southern Mainline past horse farms, Kentucky wildflowers, through the rolling Bluegrass Regions, past a 240-foot deep gorge and on to the rugged terrain of the Kentucky River bluffs. The excursions are 1.5 hours long and are narrated. The depot museum is dedicated to the construction, restoration and preservation of the railroad arts and artifacts. Their theme train rides are the best way for younger children to enjoy the long ride (esp. the Clown Days) unless you ride during naptime!

JOUETT HOUSE

255 Craig Creek Road (Off McGowan's Ferry Road west, KY 1064)

Versailles 40383

- ❏ Activity: Museums
- ❏ Phone: (859) 873-7902
- ❏ Hours: Wednesday 11:00am-1:00pm, Saturday-Sunday Noon-5:00pm (April-October)
- ❏ Admission: FREE

Have you ever heard of the "Paul Revere of the South"? Well, by touring the 1798 home of Captain Jack Jouett, you'll learn how he reportedly rode horseback for 40 miles to Charlottesville, VA to warn delegates of the British Invasion. The house contains three rooms with painted fireplace mantels, a stone-lined cellar, and two bedrooms accessed by a sharply turning stairway. Jouett's son, Matthew's famous paintings are also on display.

NOSTALGIA STATION TOY AND TRAIN MUSEUM

279 Depot Street (off US 60 bypass)

Versailles 40383

- ❏ Activity: Museums
- ❏ Phone: (859) 873-2497
- ❏ Hours: Wednesday-Saturday 10:00am-5:00pm, Sunday 1:00-5:00pm; closed major holidays
- ❏ Admission: $3.50 adults, $3.00 seniors (60+), $1.50 children (3-17)

A model train museum housed in a restored 1911 railroad station with exhibits of a reproduction of a 1926 Lionel train display and many children's toys. The displays are meticulously authentic to the original time period.

WOODFORD COUNTY HISTORICAL SOCIETY MUSEUM

121 Rose Hill (west of US 62 by one block)

Versailles 40383

❑   Activity: Kentucky History
❑   Phone: (859) 873-6786
❑   Hours: Tuesday-Saturday 10:00am-12:30pm and 1:00-4:00pm.
     Closed holidays.
❑   Admission: FREE

The local and Kentucky history museum displays focus on African-Americans, a photo collection of county events, and Civil War relics. The facility is housed in an old Baptist Church where the upstairs served as a balcony-type space for slaves attending services.

HARRIET BEECHER STOWE SLAVERY TO FREEDOM MUSEUM

2124 Main Street

Washington 41096

❑   Activity: Museums
❑   Phone: (606) 759-4860,
❑   Hours: Saturday Noon-4:00pm, Sunday 1:00-4:00pm.
❑   Admission: Donations.

This is where the author of "Uncle Tom's Cabin" first witnessed a slave auction (1833) described in the book. The facility shows slave life.

DANIEL BOONE NATIONAL FOREST

1700 Bypass Road (KY 801), **Winchester** 40391

❑   Activity: Outdoors
❑   Phone: (859) 745-3100, **Web: www.r8web.com/boone/**

❑   Hours: 24 hours a day. Specific hours for facilities within the
     park are listed below.
❑   Admission: FREE

T he U.S. Forest Service maintains almost 700,000 acres of
     timberland in portions of 21 counties in eastern KY stretching
from Morehead in the north to the Tennessee border in the
southeast. 800 miles of paved road and 500 miles of trails make
the natural beauty and recreational facilities accessible
(campgrounds, picnic and shelter areas, beaches and boat ramps -
most on KY 801). Some facilities featured:

❑   <u>GIANT CANADA GEESE OBSERVATION AREA</u> - largest of
     11 subspecies of Canada geese, mature ganders may have a wing
     span of 6 feet!. Observation deck and interpretive trail.

❑   <u>CAVE RUN LAKE</u> - I-64 exit 133, south on KY 801. 8000+ acre
     lake with 13 ramps, two marinas, 3 campgrounds, boating,
     swimming, horseback riding, mountain biking and hiking trails
     and fishing. Cave Run Dam is on KY 826 off KY 801 and has
     recreation facilities. The Cave Run Lake Morehead Ranger
     Visitor Center is two miles south of US 60 and has exhibits and a
     video presentation about the lake area. (606) 784-5624 from
     8:00am-4:30pm Memorial day thru October and open weekdays
     only the rest of the year.

❑   <u>PIONEER WEAPONS HUNTING AREA</u> - US 60, south on
     KY 211 at Salt Lick to Rd. 129. Over 7000 acres full of hiking
     and primitive weapons (only!) hunting of deer, turkey, grouse,
     squirrel, fox and raccoon. (606) 784-6428.

❑   <u>SHELTOWEE TRACE NATIONAL RECREATION TRAIL</u> -
     almost 300 miles of trails. Sheltowee means " Big Turtle" and
     was the Indian name given Daniel Boone by the Shawnee who
     adopted him as the son of Blackfish, the great Indian war chief.

Daniel Boone National Forest – Red River Gorge (cont.)

❏   RED RIVER GORGE - Mountain Pkwy. Exit 33 at Slade is
      27,000 acres of spectacular boulder-strewn areas of woodland,
      streams and waterfalls, sandstone cliffs, overlooks, arches, the
      Nada old logging railroad tunnel, and rare plant and animal life.
      The Visitor Info Station is the Gladie Historic Site (606) 663-
      2852, on KY 715, and has info on recreation in the Forest. Open
      daily 10:00am-6:00pm (April-October). The Gladie Historic Site
      is a restored log cabin (c. 1880) with displays of early logging
      and farm life and many seasonal events. Here you'll find more
      information on the 38 miles of 150 sandstone arches - Gray's
      Arch on KY 15E being a stop where you can picnic on the ridge.
      Clifty Wilderness off KY 15W are vertical sandstone cliffs,
      numerous arches, rockhouses (cliff overhangs used as shelter by
      primitive peoples), rippling streams, waterfalls, primitive
      camping, hiking and canoeing. Rock Bridge off KY 15W is a
      stone arch spanning Swift Camp Creek and Sky Bridge is another
      stone arch at the top of the ridge with a vista of the Red River
      Gorge.

❏   BEAVER CREEK PUBLIC WILDLIFE AREA - off US 27S in
      the west, KY 90 & Rd. 817 to the east. Hiking, trout fishing ,
      primitive camping and horseshoes.

❏   NATURAL ARCH SCENIC AREA - off US 27S. Sandstone
      arch that's 100 feet wide and 60 feet high. (606) 679-2010.

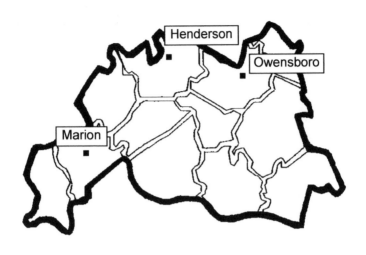

Chapter 3
North West Area

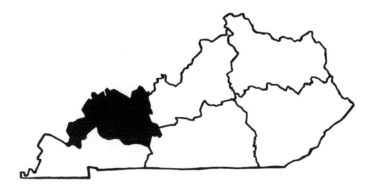

Our Favorites...

✓ <u>John James Audubon State Park</u>
   - Henderson
✓ <u>Clement Mineral Museum</u>
   - Marion
✓ <u>Owensboro Museum of Science</u>
   & Industry - Owensboro

LAKE MALONE STATE PARK

PO Box 93 (from Greenville, take US 431 south to KY 973)

Dunmore 42339

- ❏ Activity: Outdoors
- ❏ Phone: (270) 657-2111, **Web: www.kystateparks.com**

This small park is enclosed by a wonderful 200-foot sandstone bluff and hardwood forest. The park has a campground, marina, beach, rental boats and hiking trails.

MUHLENBERG COUNTY HISTORY MUSEUM - DUNCAN HOUSE MUSEUM

122 South Cherry Street

Greenville 42345

- ❏ Activity: Kentucky History
- ❏ Phone: (270) 338-2605

A museum of local history mostly focusing on the coal industry. Set in a 1912 home, there are rotating exhibits on local art too.

OHIO COUNTY MUSEUM COMPLEX

Main Street

Hartford 42347

- ❏ Activity: Kentucky History
- ❏ Phone: (270) 298-3177
- ❏ Hours: Monday-Friday 9:00am-4:00pm (April-October). Central Time
- ❏ Admission: $2.00

Different structures like a country store, 1838 log cabin, one-room school house, a restored L & N caboose and another building called Rusty Relics are all here together to explore county history.

HANCOCK COUNTY MUSEUM
Depot Street, **Hawesville** 42348

- ☐   Activity: Kentucky History
- ☐   Phone: (270) 295-6637, 927-6301, 927-8721
- ☐   Hours: Sunday 2:00-4:00pm (April-October). Central Time
- ☐   Admission: Donations

The building that the museum is housed in is an early 1900's wooden L & N depot which helps give you the feeling of going back to the time of turn-of-the-century family life and riverboat life. There's even a 1867 courtroom inside.

JOHN JAMES AUDUBON STATE PARK
PO Box 576 (US 41 north)
Henderson 42419

- ☐   Activity: Outdoors
- ☐   Phone: (270) 826-2247 OR 827-1893 Center
  Web: www.kystateparks.com
- ☐   Hours: Park open dawn to dusk. Center open 10:00am-5:00pm daily except Winter holidays. Central Time.
- ☐   Admission: $2.50-4.00 for Center.

Named for the first naturalist to artistically portray and protect birds - this is where he observed the subjects of his paintings from 1810-1819. Part of the Mississippi Flyway of migration, the Museum & Center seek to interpret Audubon's life through his original art, personal memorabilia, bird observation areas and the Discovery area with hands-on exhibits and educational themed programs. Be sure to look for a lovely souvenir reprint of his works - most notably the great horned owl and woodpecker series. Also found on site are campgrounds, rental boats, hiking trails, golf and mini-golf, tennis and lots of birding and fishing.

HOPKINS COUNTY HISTORICAL MUSEUM & GOVERNOR RUBY LAFFOON'S BIRTHPLACE

107 Union Street

Madisonville 42431

❑   Activity: Kentucky History

❑   Phone: (270) 821-3986

❑   Hours: Monday-Friday 1:00-5:00pm, closed holidays.
    Central Time.

❑   Admission: $1.00 (12 and older).

The restored log cabin is furnished as it was when the former governor lived there in the late 1800s. The museum displays old photos, civil War items and other 1800-1900 period memorabilia.

CLEMENT MINERAL MUSEUM

205 North Walker Street, **Marion 42064**

❑   Activity: Museums

❑   Phone: (270) 965-4263
    Web: www.clementmineralmuseum.com

❑   Hours: Tuesday-Saturday 9:00am-3:00pm. Central time

❑   Admission: $3.00

This is the area where 19th century pirates once robbed flatboats along the river. In the museum are more than 30,000 native mineral specimens. The fluorite crystals with a blacklight show is a must see.

UNION COUNTY HISTORICAL MUSEUM

1116 North Village Road (Camp Breckinridge, US 60)

Morganfield 42437

❑   Activity: Kentucky History

❑   Phone: (270) 389-1901, **Web: www.breckinridge-arts.org**

❑ Hours: Tuesday-Friday 10:00am-3:00pm, Saturday 10:00am-4:00pm, Sunday 1:00-5:00pm
❑ Admission: $3.00 adult, $1.00 students

Located in the old officer's club that was purchased and renovated by the county, the interior still contains over 40 murals painted on the wall by German POW Daniel Mayer. Also, see local history and art displays.

BEN HAWES STATE PARK
400 Boothfield Road (4 miles west of Owensboro off US 60)
Owensboro 42301

❑ Activity: Outdoors
❑ Phone: (270) 684-9808, **Web: www.kystateparks.com**

Known mostly for it's golf course, there's also hiking trails and an archery range.

OWENSBORO MUSEUM OF FINE ART
901 Frederica Street (downtown off US 60)

Owensboro 42302

❑ Activity: The Arts
❑ Phone: (270) 685-3181
❑ Hours: Tuesday-Friday 10:00am-4:00pm, Saturday-Sunday 1:00-4:00pm. Closed major holidays. Central time.
❑ Admission: Donations, suggested $2.00 adults, $1.00 children

Exhibitions include shows from major museums, prominent artists and important historical surveys. The permanent collection features 19th and 20th century French, English and American paintings and sculptures, as well as decorative arts (such as the Stained Glass Gallery) dating from the 16th century. The only fine art museum in West Kentucky. Young at Art Gallery is located in the middle of the museum and showcases changing exhibits of artwork done by children in the area.

OWENSBORO MUSEUM OF SCIENCE AND HISTORY

220 Daviess Street (off US 60)

Owensboro 42302

- ❏   Activity: Museums
- ❏   Phone: (270) 687-2732
- ❏   Hours: Tuesday-Saturday 10:00am-5:00pm, Sunday 1:00-4:00pm. Central time.
- ❏   Admission: FREE (Donations accepted).

The science aspect focuses on disciplines like astronomy, geology and botany. Cultural aspects of archeology, county history and Native Americans are explored too. Of special interest to children is the live reptile collection, the Government Education Center featuring exhibits that explain how government works, and a children's hands-on exhibit.

INTERNATIONAL BLUEGRASS MUSIC MUSEUM

101 Daviess Street (RiverPark Center)

Owensboro 42303

- ❏   Activity: Museums
- ❏   Phone: (270) 926-7891
- ❏   Hours: Tuesday-Saturday 10:00am-4:00pm, Sunday 1:00-4:00pm.
- ❏   Admission: $2.00 adults, $1.00 students and seniors.

Visit the Bluegrass Hall of Honor, a heritage theatre and new interactive exhibits.

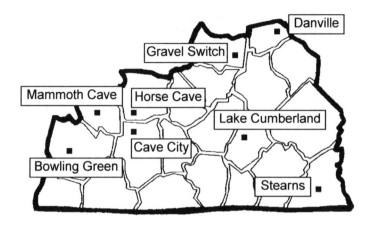

Chapter 4
South Central Area

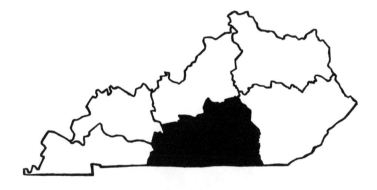

Our Favorites...

- ✓ <u>Corvette Assembly Plant</u> – Bowling Green
- ✓ <u>Lost River Cave & Valley</u> – Bowling Green
- ✓ <u>Mammoth Cave Jellystone Park Resort</u>
     – Cave City
- ✓ <u>Mammoth Cave Wildlife Museum</u>
     – Cave City
- ✓ <u>Wigwam Village</u> – Cave City
- ✓ <u>Mammoth Cave National Park</u>
- ✓ <u>McDowell House & Apothecary</u> – Danville
- ✓ <u>Penn's Store</u> – Gravel Switch
- ✓ <u>Kentucky Down Under</u> – Horse Cave
- ✓ <u>Big South Fork & Blue Heron Coal
       Mining Camp</u> - Stearns

NOLIN LAKE STATE PARK

PO Box 340 (access from KY 728 and KY 1827 north or
US 259 southeast),

Bee Springs 42207

❑   Activity: Outdoors
❑   Phone: (270) 286-4240, **Web: www.kystateparks.com**

The 5500+ acre lake is popular for boating and fishing with a
marina and beach near the park.

BEECH BEND RACEWAY PARK

798 Beech Bend Road (31W south to Riverview Ave that turns into
Beech Bend Rd)

Bowling Green 42101

❑   Activity: Amusements
❑   Phone: (270) 781-7634, **Web: www.beechbend.com**
❑   Hours: All day, daily Memorial Day-Labor Day for Amusement
     Park. Car racing is offered March - November, usually Saturdays
     at 5pm. Central Time.
❑   Admission: Water play is $2-3 per hour/day. Armband for water
     play is $6.00/day. Armband for most activities $15.00.
❑   Miscellaneous: Year-round full service campground, party
     rooms.

This is actually a multi-purpose facility offering entertainment
in car racing (stock and NHRA dragsters) and the improved
amusement park featuring adult and kiddie rides. The smaller scale
amusement park is easily family- friendly with rides like go-carts,
bumper cars, merry-go-round, giant slide, Tilt-A-Whirl, Big Mac
Truck ride, Western Train ride, Tornado, Fire House Fun Land,
Flying Dragon Roller Coaster, Deluxe Sizzler, Dizzy Dragon, Jitter
Bug, mini-golf, a water slide and swimming pool. Wet, dry, fast or
slow - you guys decide what kind of day you're in the mood for.

LOST RIVER CAVE AND VALLEY

Corner of Nashville Rd. (31W) & Cave Mill Road. (southwest of
downtown on 31W)

Bowling Green 42101

❑   Activity: Outdoors
❑   Phone: (270) 393-0077 or 793-1023
    Web: www.lostrivercave.com
❑   Hours: Daily 10:00am-5:00pm (April-October). Group tours
    available by reservation (call for details). Central Time.
❑   Admission: $7.00 adults, $4.00 children (6-12),
    $6.00 Senior (65+)

The only floating cave tour in Kentucky, it's also "re-found"
and run by some very enthusiastic, fun folks. Right under the
street is a cave with a river that "Ripley's Believe It or Not" has
claimed is the shortest and deepest river in the world. You'll begin
with the walking, history and nature portion of the tour. The cave
and valley dates back over 10,000 years ago when it provided
shelter at one time or another for Native Americans, both
Confederate and Union soldiers and the notorious Jesse James and
his gang after they had robbed the bank in nearby Russellville.
You'll also see a "Blue Hole" freak of nature for yourself and hear
the mysterious stories surrounding those who fall in it. As you
come to the cave's entrance, everyone will want to explore the
giant dance floor in the popular underground big band nightclub
from the 30's and 40's (they still have theme dances here a few
times per year and you can rent the "dance hall" for an event or
party!). Now, your group will board a long boat and the guide will
use only their hand-held light to venture into the cave. It's a small
test of nerves as you go deeper into the cave, but the guide is
careful to keep the mood "light" and talkative. An adventure not
to be missed by your family!

RUSSELL SIMS AQUATIC CENTER

2303 Tomblinson Way (at Preston S. Miller Park off of Veterans Memorial Blvd.)

Bowling Green 42101

- ❏ Activity: Amusements
- ❏ Phone: (270) 393-3249
- ❏ Hours: Memorial Day-Labor Day 11:00am-8:00pm. Central Time.
- ❏ Admission: $6.00 adults, $4.00 seniors and youth (6-17), $2.00 children (2-5).
- ❏ Miscellaneous: No outside food or drink allowed in the pool facility. Toddlers must wear swim diapers.

A newer community facility features a stainless steel 50-meter swimming pool, a zero-depth entry area with interactive water play structures like palm trees, tumble buckets and tea cups. Kids will love the splash playground full of water squirting toys such as a teeter totter, water cannons, spiral spray, water trikes and spray balls. The center also features a butterfly slide, spiral water tunnel, two double water slides and a concession area. Splash In!

WESTERN KENTUCKY UNIVERSITY

1400 Kentucky Street. Planetarium on State Street. (31-W to Western Kentucky University)

Bowling Green 42101

- ❏ Activity: Kentucky History
- ❏ Phone: (270) 745-2592, **Web: www.wku.edu**
- ❏ Hours: Tuesday-Saturday 9:30am-4:00pm, Sunday 1:00-4:00pm. These are times for museum only. Central time.
- ❏ Admission: $2.00 adults, $1.00 students, $5.00 families. FREE on Sundays. These are fees for museum only. All facilities are closed during holidays and school breaks.

W ithin the walls of the museum are the Felts Log House, Main Street: Mirror of Change, Growing up Victorian: A Kentucky Childhood and First American Roads, Rails and Rivers:

Warren County Then and Now. There's a wide assortment of prehistoric objects, pioneer relics, old fashioned toys and musical instruments. Hardin Planetarium has a 40-foot dome housing a star projector, special effects projectors and show times on Tuesdays and Thursdays at 7:30pm and Sundays at 2:30pm. (270) 745-4044 for exact show times and info. Listen for the Cherry Hall Carillon chimes in the symbolic dome on campus.

BRIMS - BARREN RIVER IMAGINATIVE MUSEUM OF SCIENCE

1229 Center Street (Downtown)

Bowling Green 42102

- ❑   Activity: Museums
- ❑   Phone: (270) 843-9779, **Web: www.premiernet.net/brims**
- ❑   Hours: Thursday-Saturday, 10:00am-3:00pm; Sunday, 1:00pm-4:00pm. Closed holidays. Central Time.
- ❑   Admission: $3.50 Adults, $2.50 Children (13 and under).

"Learn the secrets to over 30 fascinating hands-on exhibits". The BRIMS Blaster is a mini-tornado, the van de Graaf Electrostatic Generator can be "hair-raising", operating a giant interactive model railroad is easy, the wind tunnel measures air flow and you can suspend your body with the help of Magic Mirrors. Learning and fun combined at a reasonable price.

CAPITOL ARTS CENTER

416 East Main Street

Bowling Green 42104

- ❑   Activity: The Arts
- ❑   Phone: (270) 782-ARTS, **Web: www.capitolarts.com**

Their family series performances are based on popular elementary school-aged literature.

CORVETTE ASSEMBLY PLANT

Louisville Road & Corvette Drive (I-65 exit 28)

Bowling Green 42104

- Activity: Tours
- Phone: (270) 745-8287
- Admission: FREE
- Tours: Guided, Monday-Friday, 9am and 1:00pm. No cameras allowed. Closed holidays and the 1st two weeks in July. Central Time.

Since 1953, people have been drawn to the power that only comes from America's true sports car...the Corvette. This 2 seat legend has been produced here for worldwide distribution since 1982. We were absolutely amazed at the careful planning and "close-up" experiences that you'll get from this walking (1-mile) factory tour. Begin your tour with an introductory film and then see photos from famous owners from all over the world in the gallery. You'll also have a chance to win Corvette souvenirs in a trivia contest while you're waiting for your tour to begin. *(Hint: The only year a Corvette was not produced was 1983).* Once on your tour, your heads will be spinning in all directions seeing body panels being assembled and welding robots in action. Then see "the body marriage" where the newly created body meets the frame, suspension components, and its "heart"... the powerful V-8 engine. Maybe Mom or Dad will even get to start and drive a newly produced car off the line! The final highlight is watching the newly produced cars (18 per hour) enter a special glass enclosed booth for acceleration and braking tests. Hear the car's engine growl to life and quickly accelerate to nearly *100 miles per hour* and then come to a screeching halt. The car's tires spin specially made wheels in the floor which are connected to computers that measure all of the performance specifications. *Aaah...if Corvette would only make a mini-van!*

NATIONAL CORVETTE MUSEUM

350 Corvette Drive (I-65, exit 28), **Bowling Green** 42101

- ❑ Activity: Museums
- ❑ Phone: (800) 53-VETTE, **Web: www.corvettemuseum.com**
- ❑ Hours: Daily 8:00am-5:00pm. Closed only Thanksgiving and Christmastime. Central Time.
- ❑ Admission: $8.00 Adults, $6.00 Seniors (55+), $4.50 Children (6-16)

What a great way to further enhance your visit to the Corvette Factory! Especially designed for Corvette enthusiasts, you will be treated to thousands of Corvette-related exhibits and more than 50 models of every vintage, including the coveted 1953 Corvette (one of only 300 produced). You will especially love the concept cars (cars that were tested in design, but not ever produced for sale). The Chevrolet Theatre sets the stage with a high energy film about this coveted car. Experience the romance that has lasted nearly 50 years in the Nostalgia Area. Full-scale exhibits include: The Barbershop, A 1960's Service Station, 1960's Dealer Showroom, and "Route 66" which explores the feeling of spending a day with your Corvette on the open road. The Performance Area highlights the racing success of Team Corvette. Kids will love the Design and Concept Area that teaches how cars are first designed in clay through final production. Be sure to bring your camera for some great family memories! *Note: A great virtual tour is on the website!*

FLOYD COLLINS STORY OUTDOOR DRAMA

Green River Amphitheatre (I-65 exit 38, to Rt. 101 that turns into Rt. 259, watch for signs), **Brownsville** 42210

- ❑ Activity: The Arts
- ❑ Phone: (800) 624-8687
- ❑ Shows: Call for dates and times each season. Generally performances every Friday and Saturday night at 8pm. Last weekend in June - 1st weekend in September. Central Time.
- ❑ Admission charged

Come see the story of a man trapped in a cave for 16 days in the early 1900's plus other folktale productions. The Floyd Collins production is gripping and features events leading up to his entrapment and subsequent demise in Sand Cave near Mammoth Cave.

DALE HOLLOW LAKE STATE RESORT PARK

6371 State Park Road (KY 90 east, then south on KY 449 & KY 1206)

Burkesville 42717

❑   Activity: Outdoors
❑   Phone: (270) 433-7431 or (800) 325-2282
   Web: www.kystateparks.com

On a bluff overlooking a 28,000 acre lake, the modern lodge offers extreme comfort in a wilderness setting. There's great fishing, boating, swimming, hiking trails, horseback riding and mountain biking. There's also a campground, marina and a pool at the lodge.

GENERAL BURNSIDE ISLAND STATE PARK

PO Box 488 (US 27, 8 miles south of Somerset)

Burnside 42517

❑   Activity: Outdoors
❑   (606) 561-4104 or 561-4192, **Web: www.kystateparks.com**

During the Civil War, Union General Ambrose Burnside and his troops patrolled this island to keep watch for Confederate soldiers. General Burnside has gone down in history for his beard and moustache worn with clean-shaven chin - called a "burnsider"; now called a "sideburn". Most like the park for camping, fishing and boating. There's also a pool and recreation programs.

GREEN RIVER LAKE STATE PARK

179 Park Office Road (KY 55)

Campbellsville 42718

❑ Activity: Outdoors

❑ Phone: (270) 465-8255, **Web: www.kystateparks.com**

This land is where Confederate General John Hunt Morgan was captured after the Battle of Tebbs Band in 1863. The Atkinson Griffin House was the hospital set up for the defeated Confederates and now houses a battle diorama, weaponry, slide show and exhibits (Visitor's Center). Other amenities are the shoreline campground, beach, mini-golf, 20 miles of hiking trails and mountain biking. There's also a marina with rental boats.

BIG MIKE'S MYSTERY HOUSE

Old Mammoth Cave Rd (I-65 exit 53, Hwy. 70 W, straight on Hwy 235)

Cave City 42127

❑ Activity: Amusements

❑ Phone: (502) 773-5144

❑ Hours: Open daily at 9:00am. Closing times are seasonal. Central Time.

❑ Admission charged.

❑ Miscellaneous: Kentucky's largest rock shop with gifts, toys and souvenirs.

Feel the force of gravity in a strange and mysterious way.

CRYSTAL ONYZ CAVE

8709 Happy Valley Rd (off I-65 exit 53 east on KY 90)

Cave City 42127

❑ Activity: Outdoors

❑ Phone: (270) 773-2359

❑ Hours: Daily 8:00am-6:00pm (Memorial Day –Labor Day), Open from 9:00am-5:00pm rest of year. Closed January. Central time.

- ❏ Admission: $5.50 adults, $3.50 children (5-12)
- ❏ Miscellaneous: Campground with 25 primitive sites, 25 improved sites.

Crystal Onyx Cave has a variety of beautiful formations such as delicate crystalline draperies and rimstone pools. The guided one-hour tour includes a pre-historic burial site.

GUNTOWN MOUNTAIN
SR 90 (I-65 exit 53, then KY 70 west)
Cave City 42127

- ❏ Activity: Amusements
- ❏ Phone: (270) 773-3530, **Web:www.guntownmountain.com**
- ❏ Hours: Daily 10am-8:30pm, Memorial day-Labor Day. Weekends only May, Sept-mid-October. All times are Central Time.
- ❏ Admission: $13.95 day pass to everything on site (age 5+). Cave tours are $4.00 adults, $2.00 children. $8.95 adults and $4.00 children (5-11) for Town and Chair lift (Kiddie Rides and games separate).
- ❏ Miscellaneous: Saloon Snack Bar eatery, gift shops.

Howdie, it's a recreated 1880's frontier town amusement park. The town performs gun fights, a magic show, country music shows, and cancan shows (with funny antics) throughout the day. Begin your day with chair lift rides to the top of the mountain (or take shuttle bus) where the activity is. The gun fights appear to be real western shootouts with up to nine gunfights daily - each one staged differently. You never know who the bad guys are until the story unfolds. A half-hour cave tour of onyx cave is available as well as kiddie rides including a giant Ferris wheel overlooking the city. Before you leave, be sure to pay to have someone locked in the town jail ($1.00 for 5 minutes). Contact the sheriff.

KENTUCKY ACTION PARK AND JESSE JAMES RIDING STABLES

3057 Mammoth Cave Road (I-65 exit 53 to Hwy. 70 west)

Cave City 42127

- ❑ Activity: Amusements
- ❑ Phone: (800) 798-0560 or (270) 773-2560
  Web: www.mammothcave.com/kyaction.htm
- ❑ Admission: Based on activity.

P lay the western themed mini-golf course or ride the alpine slide for a thrilling quarter of a mile. Then, watch on-site glass-blowing as you lick you ice cream cone or roast a hot dog or marshmallow at the fire pit. After your snack, ride the bumper boats or exciting go cart rides. Many who visit comment that their horse riding trails are fun and well lead by guides - good for that early horseback riding experience.

MAMMOTH CAVE JELLYSTONE PARK CAMP RESORT

1002 Mammoth Cave Rd (3 miles from the Mammoth Cave entrance)

Cave City 42127

- ❑ Activity: Amusements
- ❑ Phone: (800) 523-1854
  Web: www.jellystonemammothcave.com
- ❑ Season: Mid-April - October
- ❑ Rental Fees for accommodations are $50-$100 per night with $30 fee for campsites. Most planned activities are free with stay. Large slide, mini-golf and some other more supervised play areas require a small fee.
- ❑ Miscellaneous: Joe's Diner is newer to the property and is an old fashioned 1950's style restaurant serving "grill kitchen" breakfasts and sandwich lunches. Open at 7:00am. Camp store, laundry, ice, propane, RV supplies, fast food snack shop and gift shop.

The offerings at the largest resort park in KY include: Daily visits by Yogi, Boo-Boo and Cindy; a large swimming pool with toddler pool; 350' waterslide; Yogi's petting zoo; arts and crafts; outdoor movies/bonfires; music synthesizer, mini-golf; game room; bankshot basketball; beach volleyball; small rides; batting cages; athletic fields; hiking trails; hayrides.

MAMMOTH CAVE WAX MUSEUM

KY 90 (I-65 exit 53)

Cave City 42127

- ❑ Activity: Museums
- ❑ Phone: (270) 773-3010
- ❑ Hours: Daily, Memorial Day-Labor Day 9:00am-9:00pm; March-May and September-October 9:00am-5:00pm. Central Time.
- ❑ Admission: $6.00 adults, $5.00 seniors (60+), $3.00 children (4-12)
- ❑ Miscellaneous: Next door is Huckleberry Hill Village with mini-golf, bumper cars and shopping.

Not just 120 wax figures but remarks are listed by each display. Mostly early heroes and statesmen or great stars like Albert Einstein, Abraham Lincoln, M.L. King, Elvis, Walt Disney and Jesus. Which hero is your favorite?

MAMMOTH CAVE WILDLIFE MUSEUM

SR 90 (I-65 exit 53, east on KY 90)

Cave City 42127

- ❑ Activity: Museums
- ❑ Phone: (270) 773-2255
- ❑ Hours: Daily 8:00am-6:00pm, April-October (extended 'til 8:00pm June-August). Daily 9:00am-5:00pm, Fall/Spring. Weekends only in Winter. Central Time.
- ❑ Admission: $6.00 adults, $3.00 children (3-11)

Here they have a collection of wildlife specimens from around the world - all mounted in scenes that resemble their natural surroundings. The white, cave-like hallways wind to and fro. Each of the 1600 stuffed wildlife are clean and beautiful and crisp. Look for our favorites: the reindeer, giant moose, lobster, porcupine, Kodiak bear and giant Polar Bear. This is the nicest, freshest wildlife museum we've visited in our multi-state travel.

FLOYD COLLINS MUSEUM

1240 Old Mammoth Cave Road (KY 70)

Cave City 42127

- ❑ Activity: Museums
- ❑ Phone: (270) 773-3366
- ❑ Hours: Central Time.

Near the entrance to Mammoth Cave park, it was originally an early 1930's souvenir shop. While exploring Sand Cave in 1925, Floyd Collins caught his leg. They attempted rescue, but couldn't. His death was the most widely reported news events of that time. The museum is housed in a bed & breakfast.

WIGWAM VILLAGE

601 North Dixie Hwy. (I-65 exit 53 to KY90 to US 31W north)

Cave City 42127

- ❑ Activity: Amusements
- ❑ Phone: (270) 773-3381, **Web: www.wigwamvillage.com**
- ❑ Open: March - November. Central Time Zone.
- ❑ Rates: Reasonable, most below $50 per night. Close to Mammoth Cave and Kentucky Down Under.
- ❑ Miscellaneous: Heat and A/C, private bath, tile floor, no pets, TV w/ cable, gift shop, in-room coffee. Families should request rooms with two beds or rent two teepees (or plan to camp out on the floor of the bedroom). Grills and picnic shelter outside.

"Sleep in a Wigwam!" 15 actual wigwams (a name for permanent teepees) for overnight stay. The dream of a man in the mid-1930's, they have become national treasures. This location is one of only two left open in the US. Check in at the 52 foot tall center teepee and gift shop. The gift shop has cute ceramic teepees that look just like your room for the night (be sure to purchase one as a souvenir of your stay - get one with your room number painted on it). The rooms are quaintly small and furnished with original 1930's hickory and cane furniture. Without the distraction of a telephone, you can meet your wigwam neighbors at the gathering place in the middle with a playground and Misting Deck to cool off on hot summer days. Definitely a great place to tell the folks at home about!

MCDOWELL HOUSE AND APOTHECARY

125 South 2nd Street, downtown

Danville 40422

- ❏ Activity: Museums
- ❏ Phone: (859) 236-2804
- ❏ Hours: Monday-Saturday 10:00am-Noon & 1:00-4:00pm. Sunday 2:00-4:00pm.
- ❏ Admission: $5.00 adults, $3.00 seniors (62+) and youth (12-18), $1.00 child (1-11). Closed Holidays and winter Mondays.
- ❏ Tours: Guided one half hour.
- ❏ Miscellaneous: Gardens with medicinal herbs. Stop over at Constitution Square across the street.

This medical office is a showcase to one of the world's finest collections of antique apothecary jars and equipment (did you know they used to hide medicine in biscuit dough as the coating?). Danville is the boyhood and adult home of Dr. Ephraim McDowell - the man who performed the world's first successful abdominal surgery. Jane Todd Crawford, the patient, thought she was pregnant and overdue. After diagnosing a growing ovarian tumor, McDowell suggested her only hope for survival was to travel 60 miles (on horseback) to his office. After writing a prayer in his journal, he performed the experimental removal on Christmas Day, 1809, while Mrs. Crawford sang hymns. She fully recovered, went home to her family, and lived into her 70s. Just a few of the many very unique items you need to look for are: the clock in the foyer with an arrow hole through it; the cradle that rocks and rolls; the comb-back rocker (if you have long hair you might be chosen to demo this); the little door into the "operating bedroom" with the doctor's tools laid out on the chest of drawers; in the kitchen, an old-fashioned deep fryer (french fries) or "toe" stir (toaster); or why a green jar was always placed within view of the apothecary window. We promise you'll see something here (esp. medically) you've never seen before! Very, very interesting.

PIONEER PLAYHOUSE

840 Stanford Road (US 150)

Danville 40422

- ❑   Activity: The Arts
- ❑   Phone: (859) 236-2341, **Web: www.pioneerplayhouse.com**
- ❑   Hours: Dinner served 7:30pm. Show time 8:30pm. Mid-June to Mid-August. Performances Nightly Tuesday through Saturday.
- ❑   Admission: Reserved Seats with Dinner & Theatre: around $20.00 (children under 6: $6.50). Theatre Only: around $12.00 (children under 6: $3.50)

Operating since the 1950's, this is a rustic style outdoor dinner theatre (in case of rain, indoors). The complex of wooden beam buildings serve as many pioneer shops and eateries plus each building tells a unique story about KY history. Seasonally, they perform 5 different plays - usually two of them are rated G - for family audiences (ex. All I Really Need to Know I Learned in Kindergarten).

OLD JAIL & JAILER'S QUARTERS

206 North College Street, **Franklin** 42135

- ❑   Activity: Kentucky History
- ❑   Phone: (270) 586-4228
- ❑   Hours: Monday-Friday 9:00am-4:00pm. Central time.

The county's archives are here, but, most probably come to see the graffiti and drawings by Civil War soldiers held in these jailer's quarters. A glimpse at what pioneer justice was like.

MUSEUM OF THE BARREN

207 West Main Street (South Central KY Cultural Center Annex)

Glasgow 42141

- ❑ Activity: Kentucky History
- ❑ Phone: (270) 651-9792 or (888) 256-6941
- ❑ Hours: Monday-Friday 9:00am-4:00pm Central time.
- ❑ Admission: FREE

Historic exhibits cover five counties.

PENN'S STORE

257 Penn's Store Road
(Junction of KY 37 and KY 243, across the creek/concrete bridge)

Gravel Switch 40328

- ❑ Activity: Museums
- ❑ Phone: (859) 332-7715, **Web: www.PennsStore.com** *(can you believe they have a website!)*
- ❑ Hours: Monday-Saturday 10:00am-6:00pm, Sunday 2:00-5:00pm (May-October). Monday-Saturday 10:00am-5:00pm, Sunday afternoons perchance. Their hours are "country hours" which means "give or take" a few minutes.
- ❑ Admission: FREE
- ❑ Miscellaneous: Herbal Gardens and product, Books on History of Penn's Store, Penn's Store Family Cookbook, Penn's official souvenirs, candies, homemade dolls.

A store site since 1845, in the Penn family since 1850. Penn's Store is the oldest country store in America in continuous operation and ownership by the same family. This is where the 1st post office originated on November 7, 1882 with the postmark reading, "Rollings, Kentucky" - see some memorabilia from those earlier postal years. Inside, the floor and shelves sag a little here and there. Notice the old style countertops and glass showcases or the cigar box used as a cash register. On cold days, the wood/coal stove in the middle of the store provides warmth and entices you to "sit a spell". Chances are you'll meet some locals actually shopping like their pioneer ancestors did for generations (we met the neighbor lady up the street). See Penn's Privy - it received national attention in 1992 when the first restroom facilities were installed on the site. Impromptu entertainment can stir up at any moment - whittlers, fiddlers, musicians, story tellers and singers are always stopping by to share their talents. One promise, this place will still seem unbelievable, even after you've been there! That's the word - unbelievable.

GREENSBURG BOTTLING COMPANY
108 South Depot Street
Greensburg 42743

- ❑ Activity: Tours
- ❑ Phone: 270-932-5061, **Web:www.doublecolaski.com**
- ❑ Admission: FREE
- ❑ Tours: Welcome any time during the production schedule (operations begin at 8:00am-10:00am, 10:30am-Noon, then 1:00pm-3:00pm). Central time. Children under 10 should be accompanied and supervised by an adult.

A small, family-owned soft drink bottling operation which produces "Ski", a soft drink made famous by the Kentucky Headhunters and their Grammy-award winning song, "Dumas Walker." Visitors can see a historic bottling operation still producing returnable bottles, and watching the bottles being filled, capped and cased. Most of all, children like the free drink offered at the end of the tour.

HIDDEN RIVER CAVE AND THE AMERICAN CAVE MUSEUM

119 East Main Street (I-65 exit 58, Rte. 218 east)

Horse Cave 42749

- ❑ Activity: Tours
- ❑ Phone: (270) 786-1466, **Web: www.cavern.org**
- ❑ Hours: Daily year-round, 9:00am-5:00pm. Open 'til 7:00pm during the summer. Central time..
- ❑ Admission: $6.00 adults, $3.00 children (6-12) for museum and cave. $3.00 museum only.
- ❑ Tours: Guided cave tours leave each hour from the museum. Tours may depart more frequently during the summer season.

"**V**isit the Incredible" and descend over 100 feet below the surface of the earth. Along with rushing underground water and odd-shaped structures common with caves in the area, there's also underground ruins of an 1890's era hydroelectric system. Hear the stories of how the cave was saved from pollution to become a model for conservation. The American Cave Museum is a showcase of exhibits about prehistoric cave explorers, modern cave spelunkers, cave lighting, the story of the "KY Cave Wars" (some of the funny things owners would do to attract tourists and some of the sad things that happened for the sake of exploration), groundwater science and conservation, mining and finally, a wonderful gallery of American Caves. The cave may look like others in the region but the museum is professionally done and covers all American caves - a nice add-on feature of this visit.

KENTUCKY DOWN UNDER / KENTUCKY CAVERNS

SR 235 (I-65 exit 58 to KY 235 east)

Horse Cave 42749

- ❑ Activity: Animals & Farms
- ❑ Phone: (270) 786-2634, **Web: www.kdu.com**

❏   Hours: Daily 8:00am-6:00pm, (Memorial Day-mid-August).
      Daily 9:00am-5:00pm, (April, May, mid-August-October).
      Kentucky Caverns remain open the rest of the year 9:00am-
      4:00pm. Closed Thanksgiving, New Year's Day and Christmas.
      All times are Central Time.
❏   Admission: April-October, $16.95 adults, $14.95 seniors (62+),
      $8.95 children (5-14), military w/ ID - FREE. Admission rest of
      year: $8.95 adults, $6.95 seniors, $6.95 children.
❏   Miscellaneous: Gift shops. Most walkways are paved.

This wonderful interactive nature park helps you experience Australian wildlife. Have you ever touched a kangaroo? (Discovery Area); fed a baby lamb by bottle or watched Border Collies herd sheep - you'll hear "Away" & "That'll Do" just like in "Babe" (Woolshed); learned to toss a boomerang or danced to the Aborigines Welcome song or learned circular breathing to play the rhythms of the didgeridoo? (Corroboree); journeyed thru an ancient underground passage? (Kentucky Caverns - 45 minute tours); looked at "frogmouth birds" up close?; tasted a bison burger and other "Aussie" favorites? (Outback Café); walked among emus and wallabies with Joeys? (Land Down Under Walkabout); or walked in an aviary where exotic birds feed as they land on your arm, shoulder or head? (Lorikeet Flight Cage). Wow, what an unforgettable family day! Please don't forget your cameras here.

LAKE CUMBERLAND STATE RESORT PARK

5465 State Park Road (I-65, exit Cumberland Parkway to US 127
or I-75 exit KY80)

Jamestown 42629

❏   Activity: Outdoors
❏   Phone: (270) 343-3111(lodge), (800) 325-1709, (888) 782-8336
      Web: www.kystateparks.com

Known throughout the region as one of the finest fishing and pleasure boating areas in the Eastern United States. The Lure Lodge has an indoor swimming pool with exercise room and hot tub and the smaller Pumpkin Creek Lodge is peaceful and quiet. Also available are Wildwood Cottages in the woods, nature trails, horseback riding, campground, marina, rental boats, a beach, tennis, mini-golf and recreation programs. Other points of interest in the area are the Russell Springs Visitor Center (270) 866-4333, Waterway Adventures (800) 844-8862 or www.waterway-adventures.com, Wolf Creek Dam Visitor Center (off US 27, open weekdays) and Wolf Creek National Fish Hatchery (US 127 below dam, 7:00am-3:30pm daily).

HOOFPRINTS ON THE STAIRS

370 N Spalding Avenue (Myrtledene Bed & Breakfast)

Lebanon 40033

❑   Activity: The Arts
❑   Phone: (800) 391-1721 or (270) 692-2223

A Civil War musical drama depicting Lebanon's role in the War, held in July only on the grounds of Myrtledene. Built in 1833, this Victorian home was headquarters for General John Hunt Morgan in July 1862, who once rode his horse up the stairs. Designated a KY landmark.

DANIEL BOONE MOTOCROSS PARK

775 Falls City Road (I-75 exit 41, KY 80 west), London 40741

❑   Activity: Sports
❑   Phone: (606) 877-1364, **Web: www.mxaction.com**

Motocross racing and mountain bike racing with entries from many states. ATV National every April.

LEVI JACKSON WILDERNESS ROAD STATE PARK

998 Levi Jackson Mill Road (I-75 exit 38, London 40744

❑   Activity: Outdoors
❑   Phone: (606) 878-8000
     Web: www.kystateparks.com

❑   Hours: Park open 24 hours. Mill grounds open 8:00am-4:30pm in
     the summer. Museum open daily 9am-4:30pm, April-October.
❑   Admission: up to $1.50 per person.
❑   Miscellaneous: Campground, Gift Shop, Pool, Mini-golf,
     Picnicking.

B egin with historic trails - the Wilderness Road (30 foot wide
wagon road used by pioneers) and Boone's Trace. Over
200,000 eastern settlers forged into KY wilderness between 1774
and 1796 for the promise of fertile land, abundant game, clear
streams and rivers. They faced many dangers - McNitt's Defeat
(worst KY Indian massacre) occurred here on the Wilderness Road
in 1796. The Mountain Life Museum is a log building with pioneer
artifacts such as kitchen utensils, weapons and furniture. At
McHargue's Mill you'll see a collection of millstones which is one
of the largest existing anywhere. "The people went and gathered it
and ground it in mill" - Numbers 11:8.

BARREN RIVER LAKE STATE PARK RESORT

1149 State Park Rd (I-65 to the Cumberland Pkwy, then US 31 E
south)

Lucas 42156

❑   Activity: Outdoors
❑   Phone: (270) 646-2151 Lodge, (800) 325-0057, 646-2357
     Marina, 646-2053 Wildlife Mgmt.
     Web: www.kystateparks.com or www.barrenriverlake.com

T he gently rolling hills of trees now cover the "barren" days
when pioneers came to the area and found all vegetation
burned away by Indians to promote grassland for grazing buffalo.
The lodge and cottages curve around the 10,000 acre lake with
ample fishing, boating, horseback riding, swimming (pool &
beach), hiking, tennis and caving nearby.

MAMMOTH CAVE NATIONAL PARK

(I-65 exit 53 OR I-65 exit 48, follow signs), **Mammoth Cave** 42259

❑   Activity: Outdoors

❑   Phone: (800) 967-2283 or (270) 758-2328

    Web: www.nps.gov/maca/index.htm

    or **www.mammothcavehotel.com**

❑   Hours: Visitor Center 7:30am-7:00pm (Summers). 8:00am-6:00pm
    (Fall/Spring). 8:00am-5:00pm (Winter, except 9:00am-5:00pm
    January-mid-February). Closed on Christmas. Central Time.

❑   Admission: Average Prices are $7.00-8.00 adults/ $4.00seniors/
    $4.00-5.00 children (6-12)

❑   Miscellaneous: Surface Programs - like Sand Cave Almanac with
    cave exploring, trip to Floyd Collins family homeplace - walk in
    the footsteps of tragedy. Evening Programs - 8:15pm - like Myth
    & Mysteries of the Underworld - discussion of ancient and
    modern cave myths. Miss Green River II - one hour riverboat
    tour - wind between high limestone cliffs and pass cave
    entrances. 4-6 cruises daily, April-October. (270) 758-2243.
    Moderate admission charged for cruises. Tickets at Visitor
    Center. Also fishing, boating, trails, lodging, cottages, camping
    and horseback riding.

Native Americans discovered Mammoth Cave about 4000 years ago and late 1700 settlers rediscovered the cave. By the War of 1812, slaves mined saltpeter from caves to be used to make gunpowder. The park was officially established in 1941. There are two worlds to explore - the underground and the surface world of tall-treed forests, rivers and wildlife (you'll probably see a wild turkey or deer cross your path on the way in). Mammoth Cave is claimed to be the longest cave system discovered on earth - over 350 miles charted on 5 levels! On tour, it's promised you'll learn something new. Did you know the science behind cave formations? Carbonic acid is what forms the rock (the same ingredient as in colas you drink!). Be on the lookout for troglodytes - animals adapted exclusively to darkness. Some tours lead to the Snowball Room where there's an underground picnic area. Advance tour tickets may be purchased by phone or web and then picked up at the Visitors Center at least 30 minutes before tour departure. There are gobs of people there and on a summer weekday practically every popular tour is sold out. Please make advance reservations. Plan to spend one-half to a full day here. Concessions and dining are available. With reasonable prices, try to take advantage of at least two activities. The most popular tours are listed below:

- ❑ THE HISTORIC TOUR - (2 miles, 2 hours). Best for school-aged kids who can walk for almost 2 hours.
- ❑ THE FROZEN NIAGARA TOUR - (3/4 mile, 2 hours). Good for 1st long cave tour.
- ❑ THE TRAVERTINE TOUR - (1/4 mile, 1 ¼ hours). Less strenuous version of Frozen Niagara Tour with only half sites visited. Best for young ones - probably too short and boring for older kids.

HART COUNTY HISTORICAL MUSEUM
109 Main Street
Munfordville 42765

- ❑ Activity: Kentucky History
- ❑ Phone: (270) 524-0101
- ❑ Hours: Monday-Friday 10:00am-2:00pm. Central time.
- ❑ Admission: Donations

Here you will find many Civil War artifacts, Indian artifacts, county family histories and early farming tools.

MILL SPRINGS BATTLEFIELD
KY 80W, Nancy 42544

- ❑ Activity: Kentucky History
- ❑ Phone: (606) 679-1859
- ❑ Hours: Dawn to dusk. Best to tour on weekends.
- ❑ Admission: FREE

❑ Miscellaneous: Gift shop open weekends esp. during the summer. Nearby in Monticello, Mill Springs Park where a 1840 mill still grinds cornmeal powered by a 40 foot overshot wheel. Open daily 9:00am-5:00pm,. Demos on weekends at 2:00pm (Memorial Day-Labor Day). (606) 368-8189.

Pick up the 9 stop driving or walking tour brochure as you enter the property. This is the site of the 1862 Civil War battle where Confederate General Zollicoffer fell and 203 soldiers died. See both Union and Confederate cemeteries, the area where infantry formed for bayonet charges, and the site of the Confederate field hospital.

DIAMOND CAVERNS

Rt. 255 (I-65 exit 48) 1900 Mammoth Cave Pkwy, **Park City** 42160

❑ Activity: Outdoors
❑ Phone: (270) 749-2233, **Web: www.diamondcaverns.com**
❑ Hours: Open year-round. Central Time. Closed only Christmas & Thanksgiving Days. 9:00am-5:00pm. (until 6:00pm Summer)
❑ Admission: $10.00 Adult, $5.50 Children (4-12)
❑ Tours: ½ mile long guided. Every 30 minutes, daily.
❑ Miscellaneous: Gift shop, Cafe.

This cave has been open since 1859 and is known for it's state-of-the-art lighting of the live calcite formations. As in many caverns, there's a Rotunda Room with "the Onyx Haystack" and lots of geological insight presented by the guide.

PERRYVILLE BATTLEFIELD STATE HISTORIC SITE

1825 Battlefield Road (US 68 west to US 150 west to KY 1920 north)

Perryville 40468

❑ Activity: Kentucky History
❑ Phone: (859) 332-8631 or **Web: www.kystateparks.com**

- ❏ Hours: Park open year-round 9:00am-9:00pm. Museum: (April-October) 9:00am-5:00pm. (November-March) by appointment.
- ❏ Admission: $1.00-$2.00 per person (age 6+).
- ❏ Miscellaneous: Picnicking, Gift Shop.

"I think to lose Kentucky is nearly the same as to lose the whole game…"says Lincoln. On October 8, 1862 the tranquil countryside of the area was thundered by cannon explosions and the death of more than 6000 killed, wounded, or missing. The Confederate Cemetery is where many were buried by neighbors and farmers in mounds. Perryville became the site of the most destructive Civil War battle in the state. The Museum tells the details of the battle that was the south's last serious attempt to gain possession of Kentucky. They use many actual maps, cannons from battle, uniforms and weapons to tell the story. There's also a self-guided walking tour of the battlefield park (about one mile long).

CAVE SPRING CAVERNS
567 Rocky Hill Road (I-65 exit 38), Smith Grove 42171

- ❏ Activity: Outdoors
- ❏ Phone: 270-563-6941
- ❏ Tours: Cave tours daily at 10:00am, Noon, 2:00pm and 4:00pm. Central time.

Major Native American sacred site. Nature trails, bird sanctuary, Visitor Center with art murals recreating 200-year-old Native American artworks. Tour the cathedral size rooms & passages with water cascades.

WILLIAM WHITLEY HOUSE STATE HISTORIC SITE
625 William Whitley Road (US 27 south to US 150 east)
Stanford 40484

- ❏ Activity: Kentucky History
- ❏ Phone: (606) 355-2881

❑ Hours: Tuesday-Sunday 9:00am-5:00pm (Mid-March thru December). Open Mondays in the summer.

❑ Admission: $3.50 adults, $2.00 children

M r. Whitley built the first brick house in Kentucky later named "Guardian of Wilderness Road" and had many famous visitors like George Rogers Clark and Daniel Boone. William Whitley is also noted for building the first circular track. As an expression of his anti-British sentiment, he laid his racecourse on clay vs. grass and ran horses counter-clockwise. While in the house, look for the concealed secret passageway used for escape should the house be invaded by Indians.

BIG SOUTH FORK NATIONAL RIVER AND RECREATION AREA

(I-75 exit 11. KY92). I-65 to Cumberland Pkwy. To US 27, then KY 92 west). Get map to area from Visitor's Center.

Stearns 42647

❑ Activity: Outdoors

❑ Phone: (606) 376-5073 Blue Heron

Web: http://bigsouthforkpark.com

❑ Hours: Visitors Center daily 8:00am-5:30pm (May-October). Blue Heron open 8:00am-8:00pm daily, (Summer). 8:00am-5:00pm (Rest of Year). Eastern Time.

❑ Admission: FREE

❑ Miscellaneous: Campgrounds, 150 miles of Hiking, 170 miles of Horse Trails, Picnicking, Fishing, Mountain Biking, Canoeing, Swimming, Boating. Yahoo Falls - KY tallest falls accessed by car on KY 700.

T he park encompasses 119,000 acres of wilderness, rivers and back country scattered with spectacular gorges and bluffs. Sparsely settled but once logged, you'll see remnants of industry. The Blue Heron Coal Mining Camp (KY 742 off US 27 accessed by car or railroad) is a must see in the area. Within Mine 18 is the rugged and isolated life of a mining community which operated from 1938 to 1962 and employed 300 people. Recorded voices of the people who actually lived and worked in the village tell their story from inside "shell structures" representing simple homes, a church, a school, a bathhouse and a company store that even sold jewelry. The workers were paid in script, not cash, so they had to buy everything at the company store. The Tram bridge and tipple remain - also the entrance to the mine is open and an explanation of the process is given. This is a wonderfully educational, imaginative way to study the lives of miners.

BIG SOUTH FORK SCENIC RAILWAY

21 Main Street (Parkway to US 27 south to KY 92 west)

Stearns 42647

- ❏ Activity: Tours
- ❏ Phone: (800) GO-ALONG, (606) 376-5330
  Web: www.bsfsry.com
- ❏ Admission: $10.00 adult, $9.50 senior (60+), $5.00 child (3-12).
- ❏ Tour Departure: Weds, Thurs, Fri. at 10:00am. Weekends at 10:00am and 2:00pm. In October there's also a trip on Tuesday and an added weekend trip at 11:30am.
- ❏ Miscellaneous: Whistle Stop Café, Sterns Restaurant (Coal Miners Special - pinto beans and corn bread). The McCreary County Museum of history is also in this complex.

A scenic ride to Blue Heron aboard open-sided rail cars that are pulled thru steep-walled canyons and alongside streams, pass thru a tunnel and over a bridge and into the Big South Fork River valley. Board the train at the newly restored freight warehouse (a restaurant and gift shop inside) where you can usually hear live music. The KY & TN Railway at one time serviced as the primary passage not only for timber and coal coming out of the valley, but also for the workers and supplies going into the coal and lumber camps. This is the best way to visit the stopover place - the Blue Heron Coal Camp.

OLD MULKEY MEETINGHOUSE

1819 Old Mulkey Road (KY 1446 south off KY 100 or KY 90 to KY 163)

Tompkinsville 42167

- ❑   Activity: Kentucky History
- ❑   Phone: (270) 487-8481
- ❑   Hours: Daily 9:00am-5:00pm.

Built in 1804, this is the oldest log meetinghouse in Kentucky. Many Revolutionary War soldiers and pioneers, including Daniel Boone's sister, Hannah, are buried in the church cemetery. Built during a period of religious revival, the structure has 12 corners in the shape of a cross and three doors, symbolic of the Holy Trinity.

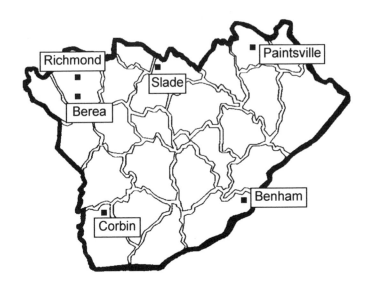

Chapter 5
South East Area

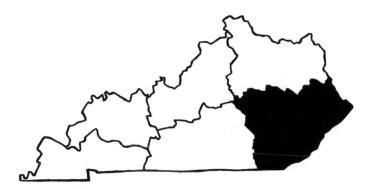

Our Favorites...

- ✓ <u>Berea College Log House</u> – Berea
- ✓ <u>Cumberland Falls State Resort</u>
       – Corbin
- ✓ <u>Harland Sanders Café & Museum</u>
       – Corbin
- ✓ <u>Mountain Homeplace</u> – Paintsville
- ✓ <u>Bybee Pottery</u> – Richmond
- ✓ <u>Ft. Boonesborough State Park</u>
       – Richmond
- ✓ <u>Hummel Planetarium (EKU)</u>
       – Richmond
- ✓ <u>Natural Bridge</u> – Slade

DR. THOMAS WALKER STATE HISTORIC SITE

HC 89 Box 1868 (KY 459)

Barbourville 40906

❏   Activity: Kentucky History
❏   Phone: (606) 546-4400, **Web: www.kystateparks.com**
❏   Hours: Daily 9:00am-9:30pm

D r. Thomas Walker was, in fact, the first frontiersman into Kentucky (he led the first expedition through Cumberland Gap in 1750). A physician and surveyor, he named the Cumberland and built a cabin, a replica of which stands on the site today. There's a gift shop and mini-golf on site too.

KENTUCKY COAL MINING MUSEUM

KY 160 - Main Street

Benham 40807

❏   Activity: Museums
❏   Phone: (606) 848-1530
❏   Hours: Monday-Saturday 10:00am-5:00pm, Sunday 1:00-
        4:00pm. Closed Holidays.
❏   Admission: $1.00-$3.00 per person.

T he building is the original coal company's commissary - now full of memorabilia from early coal mining days. Some considered camps in this area of KY "Cadillac" compared to others in the coal region - mostly because miners were treated with the respect and dignity they deserved. A guided or self-guided tour gives you a feel for what it was like to live, play, and mostly, work at this unique coal camp. Many like the exhibits of a typical company hospital, a typical miner's home, the mock mine and the tribute to Loretta Lynn, the "Coal Miner's Daughter" (with permission and personal artifacts from Loretta herself).

SCHOOL HOUSE INN RESTAURANT

100 Central Avenue (across the street from the KY Coal Museum)

Benham 40807

- ❑ Activity: Theme Restaurant
- ❑ Phone: (800) 231-0627
- ❑ Admission: Low to moderate prices. Children's Menu. Best bet is to order the special of the day.

Home-cooking style food served in a historic coal camp school. Many sandwiches are named after teachers at the school.

BEREA COLLEGE LOG HOUSE

College Square, Berea 40403

- ❑ Activity: Tours
- ❑ Phone: (800) 347-3892, **Web: www.bereacollegecrafts.com**
- ❑ Hours: (June-December) Monday-Saturday 8:00am-6:00pm, & (April-December) Sunday 1:00-5:00pm. (January-May) 8:00am-5:00pm.
- ❑ Admission: FREE
- ❑ Tours: Monday-Friday 10:00am and 2:00pm. 45 minutes to one hour long.

All students of this college work on campus in lieu of paying tuition and board - their crafts are featured at this gallery. They've been making brooms here for 80 years and weaving even longer! Visit the working studios of woodworkers (see them make the famous "Berea Basket" with all wood and paper product used), weavers (several students will make one piece - it takes two hours just to string the loom), furniture makers and broom craft (use the stalk and husk of "broom corn" - see a broom made before your eyes, then purchase it if you like). Master craftsmen supervise and teach. We were very impressed with the school's philosophies and students' attitudes about work and study! The tours are well worth the time and you'll find lots of questions to ask as you go along. Combine crafts in town with helpings of traditional KY fare at Boone Tavern restaurant operated by the college's student industries since 1909. Signature items include spoonbread, Chicken Flakes in Bird's Nest (creamed chicken served in a crisp basket of fried potatoes) or maybe try some black-eyed peas, fried green tomatoes or corn pudding. The slightly formal furnishings mean children should be on their best behavior. Entrees start at $8.00 with children's portion pricing - may we suggest lunchtime is best.

CHURCHILL WEAVERS

100 Churchill Drive (I-75 exits 76 and 77. US 25 and Lorraine Court)

Berea 40403

- ❑   Activity: Tours
- ❑   Phone: (859) 986-3127, **Web: www.churchill-weavers.com**
- ❑   Admission: FREE
- ❑   Tours: Self-guided Loomhouse tours Monday-Friday 9:00am-4:00pm (hours may vary seasonally). Closed Christmas and New Years.

Traditional loomhouse where you see the operations from warping with giant turnstile reels, weaving to finishing with accessories. This is a large scale loomhouse. Probably the largest you'll see anywhere with 50 looms. It's like playing the drums (feet and arms move simultaneously) and sounds like horses tramping over the wooden floor.

BREAKS INTERSTATE PARK

PO Box 100 (south of Pikeville on KY/ VA 80)

Breaks 24607

- ❑   Activity: Outdoors
- ❑   Phone: (540) 865-4413 or 865-4414 or (800) 982-5122
  Web: www.breakspark.com
- ❑   Hours: Park open 7:30am – 11:30pm except Winter when it's open until 6:00 pm. Visitor's Center open 9:00am-5:00pm seasonally.

❑   Miscellaneous: Sheltowee Trace Outfitters (800) 541-RAFT.
     Elkhorn Adventures Whitewater Rafting (606) 754-5080.

Sometimes called the "Grand Canyon of the South", this is the
largest canyon east of the Mississippi; over 5-miles long, 1600
feet deep surrounded by sheer vertical cliffs! A paved road leads
to the entrance of the canyon rim and there's a Visitor Center with
natural science and historical artifacts and demos of the areas
formation. Check out the parks Laurel Lake, caves, hidden springs
and Russell Fork River's falls and rapids. Hiking and rafting are
the name of the game here. Also within the park is a lodge,
cottages, campgrounds and a pool.

BUCKHORN LAKE STATE RESORT PARK

4441 Kentucky Highway 1833 (I-64 east to the Mountain Parkway, exit
    Campton and take KY 15 south to KY 28 west, then KY 1833)

Buckhorn 41721

❑   Activity: Outdoors
❑   Phone: (606) 398-7510 or -7382 (log church) or (800) 325-0058
     Web: www.kystateparks.com

Getting away from it all is easy here especially for nature-lovers,
fishermen and hikers. When staying at the lodge, you can
easily hike down to Moonshiner Hollow to the 1200 acre mountain
lake below the path. Many slowly make their way down there after
dinner in the lodge or they curl up with a good book or magazine by
the copper-hooded fireplace in the lodge's lounging area. Maybe
you want to make a side trip to Buckhorn Log Church built in 1927.
It's large pipe organ and natural white oak interior make it a man-
made natural beauty too (open 9:00am-5:00pm daily). Check out
their cottages, marina, rental boats, pool, beach, horseback riding
trails and tennis and recreation programs.

WOLFE COUNTY HISTORICAL MUSEUM

Main Street, off the Mountain Pkwy.

Campton 41301

- ❏   Activity: Kentucky History
- ❏   Phone: (606) 668-3113
- ❏   Hours: 2:00-4:00pm Sundays

Located in a renovated firehouse, there are plenty of displays of pioneer farm equipment and household items.

MEADOWGREEN PARK BLUEGRASS MUSIC HALL

465 Forge Mill Road (I-64 exit 97 to exit 16, Rt. 15 to Rt. 42)

Clay City 40312

- ❏   Activity: The Arts
- ❏   Phone: (606) 663-9008
     Web: http//members.chapel.com/hfoby

26 shows of family style bluegrass music (some performed by youth) performed in the hills.

CUMBERLAND FALLS STATE RESORT PARK

7351 State Route 90 (I-75 exit Corbin to US 25W, then to KY 90)

Corbin 40701

- ❏   Activity: Outdoors
- ❏   Phone: (606)528-4121 or (800) 325-0063 reservations
     Web: www.kystateparks.com
- ❏   Hours: 6:00am-Midnight. Until 3:00am the 2 days before, after and including a full moon. Eastern Time.
- ❏   Admission: FREE. Charge for boat rides.
- ❏   Tours: Rainbow Mist Ride to the Base of Falls (800) 541-7238. Sheltowee Trace Outfitters boat trips (800) 541-RAFT.

❑   Miscellaneous: Dupont Lodge with dining, Cottages, Campground, Gift Shop, Pool, Horseback Riding, Tennis, Picnicking, Rafting.

The "Niagara of the South" is a 125 foot wide curtain of water falling 60 feet - dramatic night and day. Dawn to dusk viewing is better for photos and safety. However, it is best to visit at night when there's a full moon. Then, you hopefully will get to see the famous moonbow (arch of light and colors), a phenomena not found anywhere else in the Western Hemisphere! How outstanding and romantic (esp. for night owls)! The Museum (at lodge) features Native American artifacts and exhibits relating to plants, animals and history from the area. Eagle Falls are nearby and are a beautifully high stream of water (vs. a roaring gush). There's also a Nature Preserve and the Moonbow Trail connects to the Daniel Boone National Forest. We find many families like to stay overnight at the lodge (<u>very family friendly</u> with family activities throughout the first floor Great Room area) and wander or hike in the daytime. The Falls are within long walking distance for grade-schoolers and strollers, but there are some hills.

HARLAND SANDERS CAFÉ & MUSEUM

US 25W (I-75 exit 29, US 25E south to US 25W)

Corbin 40701

❑   Activity: Museums

❑   Phone: (606) 528-2163

     Web:www.chickenfestival.com/sanders.htm

❑   Hours: Open daily 9:30am-10:00pm.

❑   Admission: FREE

Eat where it all began! The original Kentucky Fried Chicken Restaurant serves KFC products in the large restored dining room. See the Colonel's kitchen as it was in 1940 (early dishwashers, french fry press) when he developed his secret recipe. The business flourished because he combined good cooking, hard work and showmanship. Be sure to look in the display case for the cooking clock with the third hand. Also see his office, model motel room he rented and much of his marketing strategies. Do you know how many herbs and spices are in his chicken recipe? Did you know it was his honor system franchise concept (that he sold across country) that, at age 65+, made him money - and not his own restaurant?

KINGDOM COME STATE PARK

Box M (off US 119N)

Cumberland 40823

❑   Activity: Outdoors
❑   Phone: (606) 589-2479, **Web: www.kystateparks.com**

This is Kentucky's highest state park on the crest of Pine Mountain. The park's name was taken from John Fox Jr.'s famous novel "The Little Shepherd of Kingdom Come" a book about an orphaned youth and his journey through the hills and into the Civil War. This book was the first book to sell one million copies. See natural, unusual rock formations like Log Rock, a natural sandstone bridge, and Raven Rock, a 290 foot rock at a 45-degree angle. The popular Little Shepherd Trail (Harlan to Winterburg) is recommended for hikers and slow vehicles. There's a campground, pedal boats and 5 miles of hiking trails.

ELKHORN CITY RAILROAD MUSEUM

100 Pine Street

Elkhorn City 41522

❑   Activity: Museums
❑   Phone: (606)754-5080, (606)639-3095
❑   Hours: Tuesday, Friday, Saturday, Sunday 9:00am-4:00pm
❑   Admission: Donations

See how the railroad made its way into the area with photos, tools, uniforms, and instruments used on the railroad. Speak to retired railroad employees on the history of the railroad locally.

HENDERSON SETTLEMENT
KY 90 (16 miles southwest of Pineville)
Frakes 40940

- Activity: Tours
- Phone: (606) 337-3613
- Hours: Craft shop M-F 8:00-4:30, Saturday by appointment.
- Tours: 8:30, 10:00am, 1:00 & 3:00pm

Tours of the 1,300-acre mission include the demonstration farm, with its greenhouse, orchards and vegetable gardens.

PINE MOUNTAIN SETTLEMENT
36 KY 510 (at KY 221 & KY 510)
Harlan 40831

- Activity: Museums
- Phone: (606) 558-3571, **Web: www.kih.net/pinemountain**

Nestled in the mountains near Harlan, 800 acres of forests and fields invite you to learn folklore and the heritage of this settlement school through hands-on courses. Local mountain craftsmen help you make and take home treasures. Native stone and wood buildings provide a beautiful setting for a retreat.

PERRY COUNTY HISTORICAL MUSEUM
BOBBY DAVIS MUSEUM
234 Walnut Street
Hazard 41701

- Activity: Kentucky History
- Phone: (606) 439-4325
- Hours: Monday-Friday 8:00am-4:00pm
- Admission: FREE

The museum and gardens showcase local and county history - especially coal and lumber.

HINDMAN SETTLEMENT SCHOOL

KY 160 (off KY 80 one mile)

Hindman 41822

- ❏ Activity: Museums
- ❏ Phone: (606) 785-5475
- ❏ Admission: FREE
- ❏ Tours: Monday-Friday 8:00am-5:00pm

Hindman Settlement School was founded in 1902 on the forks of Troublesome Creek. Folk dance evenings and workshops on Appalachian culture are offered. A 12 minute video is shown on the history of the school.

FRONTIER NURSING SERVICE

KY 80 (US 421 off Daniel Boone Pkwy.)

Hyden 41749

- ❏ Activity: Museums
- ❏ Phone: (606) 672-2317
- ❏ Hours: By Appointment.

At the oldest school of nurse-midwifery (est. 1925) you'll see the Mary Breckenridge Hospital and nursing schools and centers.

BREATHITT COUNTY MUSEUM

336 Broadway Street

Jackson 41339

- ❏ Activity: Kentucky History
- ❏ Phone: (606) 666-4159
- ❏ Hours: Monday-Friday 8:00am-4:00pm

County history featuring quilting looms, spinning wheels, Civil War artifacts, and exhibits on logging and coal mining.

PORTAL 31 WALKING TOUR
US 160 (2 miles east of Benham)

Lynch 40855

❑   Activity: Tours
❑   Phone: (606) 848-1530

An outdoors tour of the 1920 coal mine and buildings. The walking tour includes the 1920 coal tipple (small-size "train conveyor" - the largest in the world at that time), the Lamp House (where miners checked in and picked up lights and mine numbers), the original post office, a depot, school, firehouse and, best of all, the mine portal (entrance). Built by US Steel, it was once the largest coal camp in the world with 1000+ structures.

BELL COUNTY HISTORICAL MUSEUM & COAL HOUSE
242 North 20th Street (US 25E)

Middlesboro 40965

❑   Activity: Museums
❑   Phone: (606) 242-0005 or (800) 988-1075
❑   Hours: Monday, Wednesday and Friday from 10:00am-2:00pm.
     Coal House open Monday-Friday 8:00am-4:00pm.
❑   Admission: FREE

Obviously, the focus is on coal mining. Bell County photos, artifacts and the 1926 house built out of 40 tons of bituminous coal.

CUMBERLAND GAP NATIONAL HISTORICAL PARK
PO Box 1848 (US 25E south)

Middlesboro 40965

❑   Activity: Outdoors
❑   Phone: (606) 248-2817

❑   Hours: Visitor's Center 8:00-5:00 daily. Park open 'til dusk.
❑   Admission: FREE

G o back in time when the gap - a natural passage through the
  mountain barrier - had been used by Indians, and then
discovered by explorer Dr. Thomas Walker. Daniel Boone and
John Finley followed in 1769 - Boone and his axmen making the
first trail named the Wilderness Road. By the late 1700's, over
10,000 settlers had come west through the Cumberland Gap. The
park is the largest National Historical Park in the country with over
20,000 acres. Start by viewing the orientation programs available
at the Visitor Center. Look over the pictures here and then see for
yourself the Pinnacle Overlook (panoramic view of three states) or
Fort McCook (built by Confederate forces to guard the gap during
the Civil War). A hiker's paradise - 80% of the park has unpaved
roads (be sure to check the length and difficulty of trails - stick to
nature trails close to paved roads for the kids). The Wilderness
Road Campground has 160 campsites for tents or RVs, a restored
log cabin at Martin's Fork (a KY Wild River), and all day hike or 4
hour shuttle tour to the Hensley Settlement (a restored Appalachian
community that flourished in isolation years ago - guided tours - if
your family has endurance of the all-day hiking or several hours of
driving to get there).

LOST SQUADRON MUSEUM

1400 Dorchester Avenue Middlesboro Airport, **Middlesboro** 40965

❑   Activity: Museums
❑   Phone: (606) 248-1149
❑   Hours: Daily 8:00am-5:00pm
❑   Admission: FREE

T he "Glacier Girl" is the plane to see here. It's a restored World
  War II P-38 fighter plane recovered in Greenland in 1992.
The displays surrounding the plane tell stories about the landing
and recovery and restoration in progress.

MOUNTAIN HOMEPLACE

(US 23 to KY 40 west to SR 2275 north, near Paintsville Lake)

Paintsville 41240

❑   Activity: Kentucky History

❑   Phone: (606) 297-1850 or (800) 542-5790 Tourism
     Web: www.varney.net/paintsville/chamber/home.htm

❑   Hours: Wednesday-Saturday 9:00am-5:00pm, Sunday 1:00-
     5:00pm. (April – October)

❑   Admission: $6.00 adults, $5.00 seniors (55+), $4.00 children (6-17)

❑   Miscellaneous: Gift Shop and Crafts Store and an Auditorium.
     Before you tour, be sure to watch an informative introduction
     movie "The Land of Tomorrow" - narrated by the famous actor
     Richard Thomas whose ancestral roots are linked to the area.
     Many structures here are original.

Trained guides in period clothing demo skills and crafts - most activities are centuries old. The family farm area has giant oxen, goats, pigs, and chickens. The farm house was the center of family life and everything was self-contained. They grew crops and raised animals for food and crafted their housewares. The Church was the center of early pioneer settlements and the hardworking families took time out each month to gather and share and nurture one another. In the one-room schoolhouse you better behave so you don't get the "board of education". The blacksmith shop has "horse-tails" to tell. Did you know there were no outhouses and no toilet paper around in those days? Pick you favorite tree, mark it and find a nice big leaf! You'll soon discover these simple, harsh lives were only happy through worship and music. Impromptu concerts on the porch are easy to spot - just listen to the "pickers and grinners" playing music from the hills.

PAINTSVILLE LAKE STATE PARK

PO Box 726 (US 460 off KY 40)

Paintsville 41240

❏   Activity: Outdoors
❏   Phone: (606) 297-5253, **Web: www.kystateparks.com**

L ots of water for boating, skiing and fishing at yet another state park with abundant water areas. Along the 1140 acres of lake are wooded coves and steep cliffs that provide the background scenery for pristine water activities. There's a full service marina with rental houseboats, pontoons and fishing boats too.

PINE MOUNTAIN STATE RESORT PARK

1050 State Park Road (off US 25E)

Pineville 40977

❏   Activity: Outdoors
❏   Phone: (606) 337-3066 or (800) 325-1712
      Web: www.kystateparks.com

W ith 27 miles of trails leading through the valleys of the Kentucky Ridge State Forest. The trails are so popular, they have been given names like Hemlock Garden, Little Shepherd, Honeymoon Falls, Living Stairway and Rock Hotel. Chained Rock is a huge chain anchored to a boulder that seems to hold it in place. The resort lodge is on a mountaintop and cottages are available too. In a natural cove in the forest lies the Laurel Cove Amphitheater open for entertainment and festivals. There's also a campground, pool and mini-golf.

JENNY WILEY STATE RESORT PARK

75 Theatre Court (US 23/460 exit SR 3 east), **Prestonsburg** 41653

- ❏ Activity: Outdoors
- ❏ Phone: (606) 886-2711 or (800) 325-0142 reservations
  Web: www.kystateparks.com
- ❏ Hours: Open dawn to dusk.
- ❏ Admission: Free
- ❏ Miscellaneous: Lodge with dining room, Cottages, Campground, Gift Shop, Marina with boat launch and rentals, Pool, 10.25 miles of Hiking Trails, Picnicking.

Ride the Mountain Parkway Skylift on Sugar Camp Mountain 4700 ft. to the top (daily Memorial Day weekend-Labor day, Weekends in the Spring & Fall). The Nature Center has local wildlife, native plants, animals and local history. Named for a brave pioneer woman, Jenny Wiley (who was taken captive by Indians in 1789). Wiley endured the loss of her children and brother yet escaped after eleven months of captivity and then started a new family and raised them - living 'til 72 years old. Weave thru the trails along Dewey Lake as your family pretends to imagine what a pioneer heroine must have endured.

JENNY WILEY THEATRE

121Theatre Court (US 23/460 exit SR 3 east, in Jenny Wiley State Resort Park), **Prestonsburg** 41653

- ❏ Activity: The Arts
- ❏ Phone: (606) 886-9274 or (877)CALL-JWT
  Web: www.jwtheatre.com
- ❏ Hours: Tuesday-Sunday, mid-June to mid-August. Youth productions Wednesdays and Saturdays.
- ❏ Admission: Free theatre in the park by youth on Wednesdays and Saturdays at 11:30am. Regular productions are $8.00-$15.00.
- ❏ Miscellaneous: Broadway musicals and the story of "The Legend of Jenny Wiley". Youth productions feature the story of "Family Feud: The Saga of the Hatfields and McCoys".

KENTUCKY OPRY

Performances at the Mountain Arts Center (off US 23 South)

Prestonsburg 41653

❑   Activity: The Arts
❑   Phone: (606) 889-9125 or (888) 622-2787
   Web: www.macarts.com

F amily entertainment with programs of country, bluegrass, pop and gospel year-round.   Look for "Munroe" the goofy character that is trying to get into showbiz or look for performances by students called Junior Pros.

RENFRO VALLEY ENTERTAINMENT CENTER

I-75 exit 62 (US 25), **Renfro Valley** 40473

❑   Activity: The Arts
❑   Phone: (800) 765-7464 or (800) 252-6685 (museum)
   Web: www.renfrovalley.com or www.brush-arbor.com
❑   Hours: Afternoon and evening shows. Sunday Renfro Valley
   Gatherin' at 8:30am. Barn Dance on Saturday nights at 7pm.
   Museum village open March-December.
❑   Admission: Varies with production. Best to get on their mailing
   list for program offerings. County Museum admission is $5.00.
❑   Miscellaneous: RV Park. Country music, family comedy and
   headliner concerts and festivals - "Kentucky's Country Music
   Capital" 12 shows weekly, Country restaurants, Brush Arbor Log
   Shopping Village

The Rockcastle County Historical Cabins & Craft Village is here too. The log cabin museum has artifacts dating to the 1700's.

EASTERN KENTUCKY UNIVERSITY
Lancaster Avenue (off KY 876)

Richmond 40475

❑   Activity: Tours
❑   Phone: (859) 622-1000

MEADOWBROOK FARM PROGRAM - (859) 622-1310. Meadowbrook Road (off KY 52). Agricultural production, diary cattle, beef cattle, sheep, swine and cropping operations. Welcome during normal business hours or tours by appointment.

ATHLETIC TICKET OFFICE - (859) 622-2122. Eastern Bypass. Over ten varieties of sports including Collegiate basketball and football.

GREENHOUSE - (859) 622-2228, Eastern Bypass. Foliage propagation and production, rose and carnation beds.

HUMMEL PLANETARIUM AND SPACE THEATER - (859) 622-1547, Kit Carson Drive, Eastern Bypass. The 13th largest planetarium in the US with space science gift shop. Admission around $3.00+/person. Family Shows Thursday and Friday @ 6:00pm, Saturday @ 2:00pm & 6:00pm. Public Programs Thursday & Friday 7:30pm, Saturday 3:30 & 7:30pm. Planetarium equipment used to stimulate the night sky consists of a giant star ball with the capacity of projecting over 10,000 stars, multiple projections of five planets, a sun, the moon, etc. - all of these operating simultaneously with surround sound. You can also travel throughout space and see the planets from other planets besides earth. At the end of each program, see the KY night sky as it will look that night - look for your favorite constellations.

FORT BOONESBOROUGH STATE PARK

4375 Boonesborough Road (I-75 exit 95, I-64 exit at Winchester)

Richmond 40475

- ❑ Activity: Kentucky History
- ❑ Phone: (859) 527-3131, **Web: www.kystateparks.com**
- ❑ Hours: (April-October) Daily 9:00am-5:30pm. (Rest of Year) Wednesday-Sunday 10:00am-4:00pm. Closed Thanksgiving and Christmastime.
- ❑ Admission: $4.50 adult, $3.00 children (6-12). (November-March, $2.00 adult, $1.00 children)
- ❑ Miscellaneous: Campground, Marina/Boat Launch, Pool, some Hiking Trails, Mini-Golf, Picnicking, Sandy beach.

After several skirmishes with Indians and rough terrain, Daniel Boone and his men reached the Kentucky River on April 1, 1775 and began laying out Kentucky's 2nd settlement. For many years this was a fortress, stopping point and trade center. The fort they constructed has been reconstructed as a working fort complete with cabins, blockhouses and period furnishings. Resident artisans share pioneer experiences and demonstrate pioneer crafts like pottery, candle-making, weaving and cooking. Riverside trails pass native plants and unusual geological sites. Begin your visit watching a film showing the struggles of the fort - esp. withstanding a 9-day attack by Indians and Frenchmen later known as "The Great Siege". A wonderful compliment to this visit is watching "Daniel Boone -The Legend" in Fort Harrod, southwest of here. Why are the names Blackfish and Henderson also important here? Look for interesting artifacts like the Clock Rotisserie, giant corn mill, walking spinning wheel or "Pop goes the Weasel". *Note: After leaving Ft. Boonesborough (because of cramped space), Daniel and family moved to a new site just north (I-75 exit 104, off KY 418 east). They suffered many hardships here and several family members are buried at this site.*

LOU-RON HORSE SHOW CENTER
1741 Lancaster Road, **Richmond** 40475

- ❑ Activity: Animals & Farms
- ❑ Phone: (859) 624-0889
- ❑ Hours: Horse shows every Sunday at 2:00pm.

Horse shows with barrel racing, team penning, poles, boarding stables to visit, riding lessons and children's events.

RICHMOND CIVIL WAR DRIVING TOUR
345 Lancaster Avenue (Richmond Visitor Center), **Richmond** 40475

- ❑ Activity: Tours
- ❑ Phone: (800) 866-3705, (859) 626-8474
- ❑ Admission: Small fee charged for brochure and tape available (for purchase) at the visitor's center.

Follow Confederate troops on a 2 hour driving tour of the battle route of August 1862. There are six tour stations established in the approximate order the battle took place. Begin at the Top of Big Hill and on to places like Mt. Zion Church (used as a Union Hospital) to the Madison County Courthouse. After the Confederate advance, they later marched in triumph into Lexington and then took Frankfort. This was the only time in the war that the capitol of a Union state fell to Southern forces.

RICHMOND RACEWAY
US 52 E (Off Old Irvine Road), **Richmond** 40475

- ❑ Activity: Sports
- ❑ Phone: (859) 625-0142
- ❑ Hours: Saturday night at 8:00pm (May-September)

A 3/10ths mile clay, oval track with several different classes of stock car racing.

WHITE HALL STATE HISTORIC SITE

500 White Hall Shrine Road (I-75 exit 95), **Richmond 40475**

- ❏ Activity: Kentucky History
- ❏ Phone: (859) 623-9178
- ❏ Hours: (April-Labor Day) Daily 9:00am-5:30pm. (September-October). Closed Mondays and Tuesdays only.
- ❏ Admission: $4.50 adult, $2.50 children (6-12)
- ❏ Tours: Last tour begins one hour before closing. One hour long.
- ❏ Miscellaneous: Gift shop, picnicking.

The home of Cassius Marcellus Clay: emancipationist, newspaper publisher, Minister to Russia, and friend to Abraham Lincoln. Overall, he was quite a character and lived grandly (notice the larger than life doors). The restored 44 room Italianate mansion is about 200 years old and has period and heirloom furnishings, a working cookhouse, outside slave/servant quarters, and many unique features for its day. They had running water and central heating (look for the outlets hidden in fireplaces and behind little doors). How were orators (like Clay) similar to our superstars today?

BYBEE POTTERY

(US 52 east), **Richmond, (Waco) 40385**

- ❏ Activity: Tours
- ❏ Phone: (859) 369-5350
  Web: www.lexinfo.com/crafts/bybee.html
- ❏ Hours: Monday-Friday 8:00am-Noon and 12:30-3:30pm. Kilns open Monday, Weds., and Friday at 8am.
- ❏ Admission: FREE
- ❏ Tours: Group tours are best scheduled on Tuesdays and Thursdays. Self-guided looking anytime.

The oldest pottery West of the Alleghenies (established before 1845) and still owned by the Cornelison Family. When you get there you'll see it looks much the same as it did then. Dirt floors, warped wood walls and clay dust everywhere really add to the feeling. If you show up and take an impromptu tour, the potters will gladly

..swer questions while continuing their work. One potter told us the trick to centering your piece is "keeping your elbows down". We also asked about the secret to Bybee's success - Answer: Handmade individual pieces and low prices. We would agree. By the time we got there on a Wednesday morning (8:30am), every showroom shelf was empty and people were paying for their purchases. They have a ritual for shopping there - you have to witness it! Like Penn's Store, miles away, this place must be experienced in person to believe!

MAGOFFIN COUNTY HISTORICAL SOCIETY LOG VILLAGE

US 460, **Salyersville**

- ❑ Activity: Kentucky History
- ❑ Phone: (606) 349-1607
- ❑ Hours: Mostly during festivals/special events seasonally.

Several authentic log homes including a one-room school.

CARR CREEK STATE PARK

PO Box 249 (KY 15 south), **Sassafras** 41759

- ❑ Activity: Outdoors
- ❑ Phone: (606) 642-4050, **Web: www.kystateparks.com**

Camping and the beach are surrounded by mountains and sun. There's also a full-service marina, boating, fishing and rental boats too.

NATURAL BRIDGE STATE RESORT PARK

2135 Natural Bridge Road (Mountain Parkway southeast to KY 11)

Slade 40376

- ❑ Activity: Outdoors
- ❑ Phone: (606) 663-2214 or (800) 325-1710 reservations
  Web: www.kystateparks.com
- ❑ Hours: Dawn to Dusk
- ❑ Admission: FREE

❑　Miscellaneous: Lodge with dining, Cottages, Campground, Gift
　　Shop, Pool, Mini-golf, Picnicking, Weekly Square Dances at Hoe
　　Down Islands, Nature Preserve, Mill Creek Lake, Balanced Rock,
　　Devil's Gulch, saltpeter mines, a cave. Trails End Horse Camp -
　　guided horse tours, primitive camping adventures (SR 3330,
　　(606) 464-9530). Red River Gorge Geological Area is
　　spectacular in its own right!

All we can really say is WOW! Even though we researched
this place for hours before coming to visit - it truly was
amazing to hike or chair lift up to the bridge. A natural sandstone
arch, the bridge spans 78 feet long and 65 feet high. There are no
guardrails (keep a strong hold of children up there...*please*) and
we were one-third of the way across the Bridge before we realized
we were walking on top of it! The hikes to scenic overlooks and
narrow paths (Fat Man's Misery) were shorter than most, making it
very accessible for families. One trail walks you right under the
bridge too! May we suggest you try a one-way or round-trip ride
on the Natural Bridge Skylift. The Skylift takes you slowly and
gradually through some of the most beautiful scenery in the
Appalachian area. Sloped gently at first, then a sharp, steep climb
up the final stretch - it will leave you mighty anxious to conquer a
short trail (600 feet) to the bridge. One way trips are $3.00 (ages
4+) and round-trips are $5.00 for adults and $4.00 for children (4-
12). Open Easter weekend thru the end of October at 10:00 am
daily. Closing times are posted daily. The whole experience is like
a giant amusement park adventure ride!

VAN LEAR HISTORICAL SOCIETY COAL
CAMP MUSEUM

Miller Circle (KY 321 to KY 302, 6 miles southeast of downtown)

Van Lear 41265

❑　Activity: Museums
❑　Phone: (606) 789-0068
❑　Hours: Monday-Saturday 9:00am-3:00pm (March-November 15)

This former Consolidated Coal Company office building has a model of the 1920's & 1930's company town, an original doctor's office, and a post office.

APPALSHOP

91 Madison Avenue

Whitesburg 41858

- ❏   Activity: Tours
- ❏   Phone: (606) 633-0108, **Web: www.appalshop.org**
- ❏   Admission: FREE
- ❏   Tours: Guided tours are available by reservation, Monday-Friday 9:00am-5:00pm, closed holidays.

This center focuses on Appalachian culture. They produce a variety of films, videotapes and musical recordings. The highlight for children, on tour, is the stop in the non-commercial community radio station. In the on-hour room the kids can talk on the radio! There is also a visual art exhibit in the gallery for viewing and, depending on the schedule, there may be something going on in the theater or a festival in progress. Stop by on your way out to buy some old-fashioned candy or just listen in on locals at the Caudill General Store & History Center.

COUNTRY MUSIC HIGHWAY 23

Maps available in downtown Ashland or downtown Paintsville

Ashland / Paintsville

- ❏   Activity: Tours
- ❏   Phone: (800) 542-5790

US 23 in Kentucky is a tribute to Eastern Kentucky country music stars including The Judds, Tom T. Hall, Billy Ray Cyrus, Ricky Scaggs, and Patty Loveless. In Ashland, stop for a bite at the Country Music Hwy. Café. Butcher Hollow is the birthplace of Loretta Lynn "The Coal Miners Daughter" and her sister, Crystal Gayle. Located seven miles from downtown Paintsville, souvenirs of Loretta and Crystal are available at the

No. 5 General Store owned by their brother Herman Webb. Herman will give you a personal tour of the home (for $5 per person), still furnished as it was years ago. Loretta and family memorabilia is scattered throughout. Any country music fan will want to say they visited. KY 321 and KY 1107 north to KY 302 east, then follow signs off Miller's Creek.

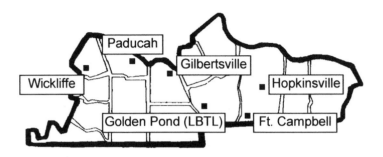

Chapter 6
South West Area

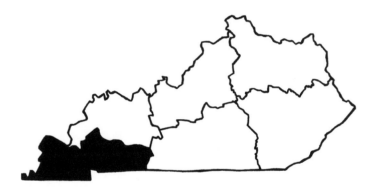

Our Favorites...

- ✓ <u>Pratt Memorial Museum</u>
    – Ft. Campbell
- ✓ <u>Maggie's Jungle Golf</u> – Gilbertsville
- ✓ <u>Land Between the Lakes National Recreation Area</u> – Golden Pond
- ✓ <u>Trail of Tears</u> – Hopkinsville Area
- ✓ <u>River Heritage Museum</u> – Paducah
- ✓ <u>Wickliffe Mounds</u> – Wickliffe

KENTUCKY OPRY

88 Chilton Lane

Benton 42025

- ❑ Activity: The Arts
- ❑ Phone: (270) 527-3869
  Web: www.kentuckylake.com/kentuckyopry
- ❑ Shows Every Friday night during the months of June, July,
  August & December. Shows Every Saturday Night Year Round.
  Central Time.
- ❑ Admission: ~$11.00 adults, ~Half-price children

This show presents some of the finest talent in Kentucky. It's wholesome entertainment for the entire family, featuring country, gospel and Bluegrass music.

LAKE BARKLEY STATE RESORT PARK

Box 790 (US 68W to KY 1489)

Cadiz 42211

- ❑ Activity: Outdoors
- ❑ Phone: (800) 325-1708, (270) 924-1131 Lodge,
  (800) 295-1878 Marina
  Web: www.kystateparks.com

The world-class lodge of post-and-beam wood construction with lots of windows for viewing is what most think of when mentioning Barkley. A spacious campground, lighted airstrip and Fitness Center with indoor/outdoor pools are favorites too. The Barkley Dam is where to watch barges going through a large lock off KY 453 near Grand Rivers and stop in the center for audiovisual exhibits relating to the steamboat era. Also cottages, marina, boat rentals, horseback riding, tennis and recreation programs.

WOODS & WETLANDS WILDLIFE CENTER

5732 Canton Rd (US 68, just east of Lake Barkley State Resort Park)

Cadiz 42211

- ❏ Activity: Animals & Farms
- ❏ Phone: (270) 924-9107
- ❏ Hours: Open year round daily 9:00am-6:00pm (you can inquire about special winter hours) Central Time.
- ❏ Admission: $5.00 adults, $3.00 children (5-12)

The park is dedicated to the conservation, education and appreciation of our natural world and they focus on many facets of wildlife.   There's a 12,000 gallon aquarium, a serpentarium with 40 different species featured, birds of prey like vultures, owls and hawks, and finally the wild mammals.

KENTUCKY LAKE MOTOR SPEEDWAY

950 Truck Plaza (I-24 exit 27 to the Interstate Frontage Road)

Calvert City 42029

- ❏ Activity: Sports
- ❏ Phone: (270) 395-3600, **Web: www.klms.com**

Dirt track racing, monster trucks, truck/tractor pulls, rodeos and occasional concerts. Many NASCAR races including late models, open wheel modified and limited sportsmen plus sprint.

COLUMBUS-BELMONT STATE PARK

PO Box 9 (36 miles southwest of Paducah on KY 80)

Columbus 42032

- ❏ Activity: Outdoors
- ❏ Phone: (270) 677-2327, **Web: www.kystateparks.com**
- ❏ Hours: 9:00am-5:00pm daily (May-September) Weekends only (April & October).
- ❏ Admission: Park is FREE. Museum is 50 cents

❑   Miscellaneous: Campground, Gift shop, Boat launches and
      marina, hiking trails, mini-golf, picnicking.

Recall the 1861 Battle of Belmont and the fight to control this
important waterway called the "Gibraltar of the West". But a
General named Grant outflanked the "Gibraltar" and forced its
evacuation. See the massive chain and anchor used by the South
to block passage of the Union gunboats and the earthen trenches
dug to protect almost 20,000 Confederate troops. The museum
was once a Civil War hospital but now serves as a display of
Indian artifacts and Civil War relics. A video is shown.

PENNYRILE FOREST STATE RESORT PARK

20781 Pennyrile Lodge Road (KY 109N, 20 miles NW of Hopkinsville)

Dawson Springs 42408

❑   Activity: Outdoors
❑   Phone: (800) 325-1711, (270) 797-3421 lodge
      Web: www.kystateparks.com

Named for the Pennyroyal plant found in the surrounding
woodlands, the place is good for a rustic get-a-way by lodge or
cottage. Also mountain biking trails, campground, gift shop, boat
rentals, hiking trials, tennis, mini-golf, and recreation programs.

LYON COUNTY MUSEUM - ROSE HILL

106 Chestnut Street (KY 730), **Eddyville** 42038

❑   Activity: Kentucky History
❑   Phone: (270) 388-9986
❑   Hours: Wednesday-Sunday 1:00-4:00pm (May 15-October 15).
      Central Time
❑   Admission: $2.00

A two story Federal brick mansion overlooking Lake Barkley
was built by the grandfather of humorist Irvin S. Cobb. The
best feature is the working model of an iron furnace.

VENTURE RIVER WATER PARK

280 Park Place (I-24 exit 40), **Eddyville** 42038

- ❑ Activity: Amusements
- ❑ Phone: (270) 388-7999
- ❑ Hours: Daily 10:00am-7:00pm (Summers). Central Time
- ❑ Admission: $13.00 average general admission. Seniors are half of the adult price.

With kiddie rides added to five body slides, two tube slides, a Wave Pool, cyclone, kiddie pool, Frog Island, action river, and beach volleyball - there's plenty of summertime fun.

MINERAL MOUND STATE PARK

(off US62/641, KY 93 south of Eddyville, north of the I-24 exit)

Eddyville 42044

- ❑ Activity: Outdoors
- ❑ Phone: (800) 325-0146, **Web: www.kystateparks.com**

On the shores of Lake Barkley, this park is historically linked to the author F. Scott Fitzgerald - this was once the farm of Fitzgerald's wife's grandfather. Boat launch.

JEFFERSON DAVIS MONUMENT STATE HISTORIC SITE

PO Box 157 (US 68 east), **Fairview** 42221

- ❑ Activity: Outdoors
- ❑ Phone: (270) 886-1765
- ❑ Hours: Daily 9:00am-5:00pm (May-October).
- ❑ Admission: $2.00

The name Jefferson Davis is best known as the man elected President of the Confederate States of America in 1861 preceding the Civil War. Ironically, both Davis and Abraham Lincoln were born in Kentucky in log cabins within one year and 100 miles apart. A 351 obelisk marks the birthplace of Jefferson

Davis, born here on June 3, 1808. The monument features an elevator to the top of the structure for a panoramic view of the surrounding countryside.

DON F. PRATT MEMORIAL MUSEUM

Bldg. 5702, Tennessee Ave. (Ft. Campbell, US 41A, Gate 4 entrance)

Fort Campbell 42241

- ❑ Activity: Museums
- ❑ Phone: (270) 798-3215, **Web: www.campbell.army.mil/pratt**
- ❑ Hours: Daily 9:30am-4:30pm, Wednesday-Saturday. Closed Christmas and New Years. Central Time
- ❑ Admission: FREE
- ❑ Miscellaneous: Ft. Campbell is home to the 101st Airborne Division (known as the "Screaming Eagles"), the 5th Special Forces Group and the 160th Special Operations Aviation Regiment

Probably the best thing to check out is the WW II cargo gliders displayed on this large military reservation dedicated museum. Exhibits on the history of Ft. Campbell and the many units stationed here from the present back to World War II include: uniforms, photos, restored aircraft and some weapons. There's even a display with Adolph Hitler's walking stick.

MAGGIE'S JUNGLE GOLF

7301 US Hwy 641 N (near Kentucky Dam), **Gilbertsville 42044**

- ❑ Activity: Outdoors
- ❑ Phone: (270) 362-8933,
- ❑ Hours: Call for seasonal hours.

Putt-putt at its best. Enjoy a combination of shuffleboard, putt-putt and live animals with a petting zoo, nature trail, covered bridges and a picnic area or take a ride in the Safari Car. The nature trail has pygmy goats, llamas, pot-bellied pigs, zonie, camel, miniature horses.

KENTUCKY DAM VILLAGE

PO Box 69 (I-24 east to US 62 to US 641east), **Gilbertsville 42044**

❑   Activity: Outdoors
❑   Phone: (270) 362-4271 Lodge, (800) 325-0146,
         (270) 362-8386 Marina, **Web:www.kystateparks.com**

This is one of three resort parks surrounding Land Between the Lakes National Recreation Area. With an abundance of water, the most popular sports are boating, water-skiing, snorkeling and fishing. The main lodge has private balconies or patios and fine dining. There's also cottages, campground, gift shop, airport, marina, boat rentals, pool, beach, tennis, mini-golf and recreation programs.

LAND BETWEEN THE LAKES NATIONAL RECREATION AREA

100 Van Morgan Drive (I-24w exit 31, KY 453 south to the Trace on US 68/KY80 between Kentucky Lake and Lake Barkley)

Golden Pond 42211

❑   Activity: Outdoors
❑   Phone: (270) 924-2020, **Web: www.lbl.org**
❑   Hours: Open year-round but some facilities are closed during
         winter. See specific facility hours below. Central Time
❑   Admission: FREE, except specific facilities listed below.
❑   Miscellaneous: Kentucky Kayak Kountry Phone: 270-362-0081

"Land Between the Lakes" located between:

❑   KENTUCKY LAKE - a top fishing , water sport and water
         recreation areas on the largest lake in KY. Over 2300 miles of
         shoreline with the KY Dam (US 62/641) at Gilbertsville across
         the Tenn. River is 208 ft. high and 8400 ft. wide.
❑   LAKE BARKLEY - 2nd largest KY lake with 1000 miles of
         shoreline for recreation and the water for fishing. The Barclay
         Dam is off KY 453 near Grand Rivers across the Cumberland
         River.

Facilities available:

- **GOLDEN POND VISITORS CENTER** - centrally located, has info, displays, a planetarium and video orientation. Open 9:00am-5:00pm, year-round, except Thanksgiving, Christmas and New Year's. Planetarium admission is between $2-$3.

- **ELK & BISON PRAIRIE** - 1 mile north on the Trace. 750 acre preserve is a recreation of the prairie that existed over 200 years ago - mostly grassland and American Indian era animals like bison, elk, deer, wild turkeys, coyotes, rabbits, hawks, owls and songbirds. A drive-thru park with interpretive displays at various spots. Daily dawn-dusk. Admission $3.00 per vehicle.

- **THE HOMEPLACE** - 15 miles south on the Trace. A living-history farm which re-creates the farming and daily activities of a typical rural family living between the Cumberland and Tennessee rivers in the 1850s. Interpreters are dressed in period clothing and talk to guests while doing daily chores. There are 16 buildings (some original), an interpretive center with exhibits and video orientation, and many seasonal festivals most every weekend. Monday-Saturday 9:00am-5:00pm, Sunday 10:00am-5:00pm (April-October); Closed Mondays and Tuesdays in March and November. Admission $3.50 adults, $2.00 children (5-12).

- **THE NATURE STATION** - north on the Trace, then east on Mulberry Flat Road, follow signs. An environmental education center offering canoe rentals, trails and live animal exhibits. Special weekend events March thru November. Bald eagle viewing excursions by boat and van in the winter months. Open Monday-Saturday 9am-5pm, Sunday 10am-5pm (April-October); Closed Mondays and Tuesdays in March and November. Area is FREE but Nature Station is $3.50 adults, $2.00 children (5-12).

PATTI'S 1880'S SETTLEMENT

1793 J.H. O'Bryan Drive (I-24 exit 31 south)

Grand Rivers 42045

❑   Activity: Theme Restaurant
❑   Phone: 270-362-8844, 888-736-2515
    Web:www.pattis-settlement.com
❑   Hours: Open daily 10:30am-8:00pm. Central time.
❑   Moderate prices. Children's menu.

R elaxed dining in 1880s atmosphere featuring homemade pies, flower pot bread and 2" thick pork chops. Historic log cabin settlement with unique shops, miniature golf and animal park. Try the mile-high lemon meringue pie, Bill's Boatsinker or Sawdust pie.

ROBERT PENN WARREN BIRTHPLACE MUSEUM

Corner of Third and Cherry Streets

Guthrie 42234

❑   Activity: Museums
❑   Phone: (270) 483-2683
❑   Hours: Tuesday-Saturday 11:30am-3:30pm, Sunday 2:00-
    4:00pm. Closed holidays. Central time.
❑   Admission: Donations

H ere is the boyhood home of America's first poet laureate, Robert Penn Warren, author of 10 novels and 16 volumes of poetry. Warren lived here in the early 1900's until age 16. Inspire your children by viewing photos, books and works of the author on display.

HARDIN SOUTHERN RAILROAD

KY 80 (KY 80 east of US 641soutt)

Hardin 42048

- ❑ Activity: Tours
- ❑ Phone: (270) 437-4555, **Web: www.hsrr.com**
- ❑ Admission: ~$10.00 adults, $6.00 children (3-12)
- ❑ Tours: Saturday twice in the afternoon and Sunday departure around 1:15pm (Memorial Day - end of October). Central Time. Seasonal theme rides too (see seasonal chapter).
- ❑ Miscellaneous: Railroad Diner Restaurant open in the summer for light lunch and full dinner. Moderate pricing.

A n 18-mile nostalgic excursion through the beautiful Clarks River Valley on a 100+ year old railroad. Sit in reclining seats with climate controlled coaches while watching for forest and farmland along your 2 hour journey.

KENLAKE STATE RESORT PARK

542 Kenlake Road (I-24 north, exit US 68/KY 80W OR I-24 to Purchase Pkwy, then US 68E), **Hardin 42048**

- ❑ Activity: Outdoors
- ❑ Phone: (800) 325-0143, Lodge (270) 474-2211 Marina (270) 474-2245 **Web: kystateparks.com**

L ocated on the western shore of Kentucky Lake, this park features an indoor tennis center and pro shop, 200 miles of woodland trails and a grand hotel. Also cottages, campgrounds, marina, boat rentals, a pool, horseback riding trails and recreation programs.

PENNYROYAL AREA MUSEUM

217 East Ninth Street

Hopkinsville 42240

- ❏ Activity: Kentucky History
- ❏ Phone: (270) 887-4270, **Web: www.commercecenter.org**
- ❏ Hours: Monday-Friday 8:30am-4:30pm, Saturday 10:00am-3:00pm. Closed all major holidays. Central time.

The colorful past of Southwestern Kentucky comes alive at the Pennyroyal Area Museum. Travel back in time to see the night riders lighting up the sky during the tobacco war...the Cherokee Indians marching along the Trail of Tears...and displays of famous locals.

TRAIL OF TEARS COMMEMORATIVE PARK

US 41 South,

Hopkinsville 42240

- ❏ Activity: Outdoors
- ❏ Phone: (270) 886-8033, **Web: www.trailoftears.org**

The Trail of Tears Commemorative Park is situated on a portion of the campground used by the Cherokees on the infamous Trail of Tears and includes the gravesites of Chiefs White Path and Fly Smith. The park includes a Heritage Center, picnic areas and ample parking.

PLAYHOUSE IN THE PARK

Gil Hopson Drive , **Murray 42071**

- ❏ Activity: The Arts
- ❏ Phone: (270) 759-1752
- ❏ Hours: Year-round productions are performed Thursday-Saturday evenings and Sunday matinees. Central time.

Family entertainment of comedies, musicals (like Heidi), dramas and mysteries.

WRATHER-WEST KENTUCKY MUSEUM

120 North 8th Street, Murray State University

Murray 42071

- ❏ Activity: Kentucky History
- ❏ Phone: (270) 247-6971
- ❏ Hours: Monday-Friday 8:30am-4:15pm, Saturday 10:00am-
  1:00pm. Central Time

L ocated in a renovated icehouse, this history promotes an understanding of social, cultural and economic development of western Kentucky. Many like to look at the Jackson Purchase memorabilia.

ALBEN W. BARKLEY MUSEUM

533 Madison Street

Paducah 42001

- ❏ Activity: Museums
- ❏ Phone: (270) 442-7064
- ❏ Hours: Saturday-Sunday 1:00-4:00pm or by appointment.
  Central time.
- ❏ Admission: $2.00 adults, 50c children under 12

S tudents and members of the Jr. Historians Assn. guide visitors through the exhibits housed in Capt. Wm. Smedley's 1852 home.   Exhibits honor Barkley, US Senator & Vice President (1949-53) and display local history.

MARKET HOUSE THEATRE

132 Market House Square

Paducah 42001

- ❏ Activity: The Arts
- ❏ Phone: (888) MHT-PLAY, **Web: www.mhtplay.com**

15-20 productions per season of comedy, musicals and children's shows like The Velveteen Rabbit and the Children's Choir.

MILLSPRINGS AMUSEMENT PARK

(off I-24, exit #4), 200 McBride

Paducah 42001

❑ Activity: Amusements
❑ Phone: (270) 442-2111, **Web: www.millspringamusements.com**
❑ Hours: Late morning - dark. Open daily during the summer, weekends only in April, May, September, October. Call (or check website) for updated hours each season. Splash waterpark only open summers.
❑ Admission: $10.00-$25.00 depending on the number of activities.

The wild west Kentucky has a park with rollercoaster, a few small rides, mini-golf, bumper boats, a ferris wheel and kiddie go carts. There's also Splash water park slides and pools and Wild Bill's Restaurant in the same complex.

MUSEUM OF THE AMERICAN QUILTER'S SOCIETY

215 Jefferson Street (I-24 Downtown Loop)

Paducah 42001

❑ Activity: Museums
❑ Phone: (270) 442-8856, **Web: www.aqsquilt.com**
❑ Hours: Monday-Saturday 10:00am-5:00pm year round. Sunday 1:00-5:00pm (April-October). Closed all Winter and Spring holidays. Central Time
❑ Admission: $5.00 adults, $3.00 students over 12.
❑ Miscellaneous: Gift shop and bookstore.

Changing theme exhibits display over 150 quilts from old-fashioned to modern to colorful to unique or abstract. The building has eight stained glass windows with designs based on quilt patterns.

PADUCAH INTERNATIONAL RACEWAY

4445 Shemwell Lane, **Paducah** 42001

- ❑   Activity: Sports
- ❑   Phone: (270) 898-7469
      Web: www.kraze.com/paducevents.html
- ❑   Hours: Some Friday and most every Saturday night beginning at
      7:00pm, gates open at 4:00pm (May-October) Central time.

A 5/8 mile, high bank dirt track. Racing, late model, modified, pre-stock and street stock autos.

PADUCAH RAILROAD MUSEUM

3rd & Washington Streets, **Paducah** 42001

- ❑   Activity: Museums
- ❑   Phone: (270) 442-4032
- ❑   Hours: Saturday 10:00am-4:00pm. Central time.
- ❑   Admission: FREE

Located in the upper offices of the N.C. & St. L. Railway Freight office, railroad history museum with collection of railroad artifacts and memorabilia including lights, signals, diesel control stands, hand pump car, tools, lanterns, photos, maps, books, vintage telegraph and telephone equipment, etc.

RIVER HERITAGE MUSEUM

Water Street, **Paducah** 42001

- ❑   Activity: Museums
- ❑   Phone: (270) 575-1005,
- ❑   Tours: by reservation

Overlooking the confluence of the Tennessee and Ohio Rivers stands the Center for Maritime Education. View river navigation simulation in progress from an observation deck. Interactive permanent and changing exhibits tell the story of the Four Rivers Region, a geographic area that encompasses the Ohio, Cumberland, Tennessee and Mississippi Rivers.

TILGHMAN HERITAGE CENTER & CIVIL WAR INTERPRETIVE CENTER

631 Kentucky Avenue

Paducah 42001

- ❑ Activity: Museums
- ❑ Phone: (270) 575-1870
- ❑ Hours: 10:00am-4:00pm. Central time.
- ❑ Admission: $1.50 general admission

Restored home of Gen. Lloyd Tilghman includes Civil War exhibits that explain Paducah's role in the war.

WHITEHAVEN WELCOME CENTER

Kentucky Welcome Center (I-24E exit 7, US 45)

Paducah 42001

- ❑ Activity: Kentucky History
- ❑ Phone: (270) 554-2077 or (800) 225-TRIP
  Web: www.paducah-tourism.org
- ❑ Hours: Daily 8:00am-6:00pm. Central time
- ❑ Admission: FREE
- ❑ Tours: Daily on the half hour 1:00-4:00pm
- ❑ Miscellaneous: Modern restroom facilities open 24 hours.

Whitehaven mansion was built in the mid-1800s and the historical tourist center is designed to offer a glimpse of the state's past and symbolize Kentucky's position as a gateway to the South.

WILLIAM CLARK MARKET HOUSE MUSEUM

121 Market House Square (Center of the Market House)

Paducah 42001

- ❑ Activity: Museums
- ❑ Phone: (270) 443-7759

❑   Hours: Monday-Saturday Noon-4:00pm. Closed Sundays and
     major holidays. Central Time.
❑   Admission:$1.50 adults, 50 cents children (6-17)

Articles displayed from Paducah's history in the 1905 Market
House. Find inside a 1870's drug store, Civil War relics, river
and local history exhibits.

YEISER ART CENTER
200 Broadway Street, **Paducah** 42001

❑   Activity: The Arts
❑   Phone:(270)442-2453, **Web:www.yeiser.org**
❑   Hours: Tuesday-Saturday 10:00am-4:00pm Closed January.
     Central time.

Changing exhibitions of Kentucky and national artists,
contemporary and historical art forms, painting, photography,
sculpture, prints, mixed media, fibers. National Fibers Exhibit each
spring. Call ahead for the Elements in Art handout that helps your
children understand the basics of art in every work they view. The
art appreciation card can be utilized with any exhibit that they
sponsor. The card can be used by the child alone or with an adult.
It provides information based on the elements of art, poses
questions, and suggests that the child interact (visually) with the
works. They also have interactive panels that are hands on. They
show an example of a recognized work of art and then invite the
children to draw, paint, touch, or move items to illustrate the
various concepts shown on the panels.

ADSMORE HOUSE MUSEUM AND RATLIFF GUNSHOP
304 North Jefferson Street , **Princeton** 42445

❑   Activity: Museums
❑   Phone (270) 365-3114
❑   Hours: Tuesday-Saturday 11:00am-4:00pm, Sunday 1:30-
     4:00pm. Central time.

❑   Admission: $5.00 adults, $4.50 seniors (65+), $2.00 children (6-12). Gun Shop $1.00

A c. 1857 Greek Revival home restored to late Victorian. Period-costumed guides give the feeling of that place and time. The Gunshop is restored to 1844 to tell the story of Princeton's first gunsmith.

CALDWELL COUNTY RAILROAD MUSEUM & CABOOSE

116 Edwards Street

Princeton 42445

❑   Activity: Museums
❑   Phone: (270) 365-0582
❑   Hours: Wednesday-Sunday 1:00-4:00pm.
❑   Admission: Donations

A collections of railroad memorabilia and artifacts in an old caboose.

WICKLIFFE MOUNDS

94 Green Street (northwest on US 51 / 60 / 62)

Wickliffe 42087

❑   Activity: Outdoors
❑   Phone: (270) 335-3681
❑   Hours: Daily 9:00am-4:30pm (March-November). Central Time.
❑   Admission: $4.00 adults, $3.75 seniors (55+), $3.00 children (6-11)

This Research Center and Archeological Site is where they've excavated prehistoric (1100-1350AD) Mississippian Mound culture villages. Unearthed for current viewing is a burial mound, home sites and temple mounds with different interpretive exhibits that illustrate prehistoric Indian life and also explain how the archeologists do their work.

Seasonal & Special Events

JANUARY

MARTIN LUTHER KING DAY

NC - Hodgenville, Abraham Lincoln Birthplace NHS. (270) 358-3173. Musical tribute.

NATIVE AMERICAN WEEKEND

SC - Jamestown, Lake Cumberland SRP. (800) 325-1709. Demos of Native American culture including a buffalo meat dinner. (Last weekend in January).

FEBRUARY

LINCOLN'S BIRTHDAY CELEBRATION

NC - Hodgenville, Abraham Lincoln Birthplace NHS. (270) 358-3137. The president is honored by a procession to the symbolic birthplace cabin and the placement of a wreath on the door.

EDISON BIRTHDAY PARTY

NC - Louisville, Edison's Home. (502) 585-5247. Celebrate Thomas Edison's birthday with a visit to his Butchertown home full of artifacts and tales of little known facts. (1st weekend in February).

BUFFALO DINNER AND NATIVE AMERICAN HERITAGE DAY

SW - Gilbertsville, Kentucky Dam Village SRP. (270) 362-4271. Native American cultural demos, food and dance. (Mid-February).

MARCH

KENTUCKY HILLS WEEKEND

SE - Corbin, Cumberland Falls SRP. (800) 325-0063. Expressions of Appalachian culture through crafts, storytelling and music. (1st weekend in March).

ST. PATRICK'S DAY PARADE

NE - Lexington, Main Street. (859) 278-7349. Leprechauns, shamrocks, parade.

CIVIL WAR HISTORY WEEKEND

NW - Paducah, Schultz Park an Tilghman Heritage Center & Civil War Museum. (800) PADUCAH. Living history commemorating the 1864 Battle of Paducah. Commemorative talk and interpretive walking tour, firing demonstrations, living history demonstrations of Civil War soldiers. (4th weekend in March)

APRIL

EASTER CELEBRATIONS

Easter egg hunts, the Easter Bunny, Brunch Buffet and Sunrise Service. Most State Resort Parks. (Easter weekend)

- ❑   **NC - HAPPY EASTER BRUNCH CRUISE**. Star of Louisville. (502) 589-7827.
- ❑   **NC - EASTER BUNNY EXPRESS**. Kentucky RR Museum. New Haven. (502) 549-5470.
- ❑   **SE - EASTER EGG-STRAVAGANZA**. Renfro Valley Center. (800) 765-7464.

April (cont.)

ARBOR DAY CELEBRATION

NC - Bernheim Forest, **Clermont**. (502) 955-8512. Kentucky's official research and arboretum forest is host to a weekend of learning about botany and the importance of trees. (1st weekend in April)

KENTUCKY DERBY FESTIVAL

NC - **Louisville**. (800) 928-FEST. www.kdf.org (Mid-April thru 1st Saturday in May)

- ❑ Thunder Over Louisville, riverfront. The nation's largest fireworks and pyrotechnics display on earth (1 million people)! Also a great military air show. (Mid-April Saturday)
- ❑ KyDzFest, Kentucky Fair and Exposition Center. Giant interactive playground with children's entertainment and games. (Last Thursday-Sunday in April)
- ❑ Great Balloon Race, Kentucky Fair and Exposition Center. Over 35 hot air balloons in the chase of the "hare" balloon. (Last Saturday in April)
- ❑ Bedlam in the Streets Bed Races, Louisville Motor Speedway. Evening bed races. Corporate teams race in themed beds. Parade of beds at 6pm. (1st Monday in May)
- ❑ Great Steamboat Race, riverfront. The race between the Belle of Louisville against a rival boat like the Delta Queen. (1st Wednesday of May)
- ❑ Pegasus Parade, downtown. Spectacle of colorful floats, marching bands, giant inflatables, equestrians and celebrities starting west on Broadway. (1st Thursday in May)
- ❑ Governor's Derby Breakfast, Capitol grounds, Frankfort. (800) 960-7200. Everyone is invited to the Capitol building for a free breakfast along with entertainment and crafts to enjoy afterwards. (Morning of the 1st Saturday in May - Derby Day)

MOUNTAIN FOLK FESTIVAL

SE - Berea, Seabury Center. (859) 986-4434. Appalachian culture is highlighted through instruction in Appalachian, English and Danish dance; folk games; and performances by school dance groups (4th grade to high school). (1st weekend in April)

CUMBERLAND GAP'S ENCAMPMENT OF THE SEVERED UNION

SE - Middlesboro, Cumberland Gap NHP. (606) 248-2817. How was the Gap important to the Union and Confederacy during the Civil War? (Last weekend in April)

HILLBILLY DAYS FESTIVAL

SE - Pikeville, downtown. (800) 844-7453. More than 60,000 people will show up for a fun look at the Hillbilly stereotype with food, a carnival, a parade and music that puts everyone in a "laid back" kinda mood. (Mid-April for 3 days)

MAY

KENTUCKY SCOTTISH WEEKEND

NC - Carrollton, General Butler SRP. (800) 325-0078. The state celebrates many with Scottish heritage with athletic competitions, games, contests (how about the boniest knee's contest?). dancing and food. (2nd weekend in May)

MAY DAY CELEBRATION

NC - Harrodsburg, Old Fort Harrod State Park. (859) 734-3314. Traditional celebration of dancing around a May Pole with fanfare. (May 1st)

May (cont.)

MOTHER'S DAY EXPRESS

NC - New Haven, Kentucky RR Museum. (800) 272-0152. Scenic train trip. Discounts for Moms with children. (Mother's Day)

TRAIN ROBBERY

NC - New Haven, Kentucky RR Museum. (800) 272-0152. Fake train robbery excursion. (Memorial Day)

WEST POINT CIVIL WAR DAYS

NC - West Point, Fort Duffield. (502) 922-4560. The Federals built the fort high above the town to protect an important supply depot on the Ohio River. The re-enactment takes place inside the actual fort with tours and a pretend bank robbery. (May)

PIONEER FESTIVAL

NE - Corinth, Mullins Log Cabin. (859) 824-0565. The best way to visit this cabin is during a celebration of pioneer demonstrations, crafts, food and activities. (2nd weekend in May)

DEAFESTIVAL

NE - Covington Convention Center. (800) 372-2907. Enjoy the educational and cultural activities surrounding American sign language and the deaf culture. (Memorial Day)

LADY GANGSTER TRAIN ROBBERY

NE - Versailles, Bluegrass Railroad Museum. (800) 755-2476. Lady robbers re-enactment aboard a restored train ride. (Memorial Day weekend)

INTERNATIONAL BAR-B-Q FESTIVAL

NW - Owensboro, downtown. (800) 489-1131 or www.bbqfest.com. Cooking teams compete to make the finest barbecued mutton, chicken and thousands of gallons of burgoo as judged and consumed by the public. Also games, contests and country dancing. (2nd weekend in May)

BATTLE OF SACRAMENTO

NW - Sacramento. (270) 736-5274. This re-enactment takes place on the original battlefield where Confederate Gen. Nathan Forrest and his bunch of 300 men won the day (Dec. 1861). (May)

MEMORIAL DAY CELEBRATION

SC - Lebanon National Cemetery. (502) 893-3852. Civil War military units will be in period dress to rededicate the cemetery Union soldiers from the Battle of Perryville and Tebbs Bend. (Memorial Day)

MEMORIAL DAY CELEBRATIONS

ALL AREAS - www.kystateparks.com or (800) 225-PARK. Most State Resort Parks provide entertainment and activities all weekend.

JUNE

CAPITAL EXPO FESTIVAL

NC - Frankfort, downtown. (502) 875-3524. Live entertainment, hot air balloon rides, fireworks and children's activities. (1st full weekend in June)

June (cont.)

OLD FORT HARROD HERITAGE FESTIVAL

NC - Harrodsburg, Old Fort Harrod SP. (859) 734-3314. A celebration of state history and pioneer heritage with wagon rides, music, living history re-enactments of the fort's attack, craft demos and hands-on activities. (1st full weekend in June)

SHAKERTOWN CIVIL WAR ENCAMPMENT

NC - Harrodsburg, Shaker Village of Pleasant Hill. (800) 734-5611. The Civil War as seen from the eyes of a strong, ritualistic religious community during this tumultuous period. (1st weekend in June)

EQUITANA USA

NC - Louisville, Kentucky Fair and Exposition Center. (800) 393-4913 or (888) HORSES-1 or www.equitanausa.com. The world's fair of the horse industry hosts horses and enthusiasts from around the world. 10's of 1000's of horse lovers attend workshops that showcase the latest products and services or attend the "Mane Event" where horses are dressed and shown plus Country Headliner concerts. Admission: approx. $12/day. (3rd weekend in June - Thursday-Sunday)

GREEK FESTIVAL

NC - Louisville, Fifth Street. (502) 587-6247. Authentic Greek music and dancing, authentic Greek food!, arts and crafts and kid's interactive activities. (last weekend in June)

FATHER'S DAY EXCURSION

NC - New Haven, Kentucky Railway Museum. (800) 272-0152. Fathers are half-price today.

MORGAN'S RAID ON GEORGETOWN

NE - Georgetown, Cardome Center. (502) 863-1575. 500 re-enactors converge to take us all back to the days of the Civil War. Artillery night firings, military maneuvers and pioneer food. (2nd weekend in June)

FESTIVAL OF THE BLUEGRASS

NE - Lexington, Kentucky Horse Park. (800) 678-8813. The oldest bluegrass festival around with national bands (traditional, contemporary, ole tyme string style), workshops and kids activities. (2nd weekend in June-Thursday-Sunday)

W.C. HANDY BLUES AND BARBEQUE FESTIVAL

NW - Henderson. (800) 648-3128. The legendary blues musician and composer is honored by his hometown community with jazz music and mouthwatering barbecue. (Entire 2nd full week in June)

DUNCAN HINES FESTIVAL

SC - Bowling Green. (800) 326-7465. The native son of the famous baking products is honored with activities, food (esp. desserts) and music. (2nd weekend in June)

GREAT AMERICAN BRASS BAND FESTIVAL

SC - Danville, Centre College Lawn. (800) 755-0076. "The most prominent and unusual musical festival in the country" is a FREE presentation of world-class bands. (2nd weekend in June)

CATCH A RAINBOW KIDS FISHING DERBY

SC - Jamestown, Wolf Creek Fish Hatchery. (270) 343-3797. Fishing derby for kids ages 0-15 with prizes and trophies awarded. (1st Saturday in June)

June (cont.)

GLASGOW HIGHLAND GAMES

SC - Lucas, Barren River Lake SRP. www.mammothcave.com/ highland.htm. A Scottish Heritage and Family Celebration with dancing , bagpipe and harp competition and children's games. (weekend after Memorial Day - Thursday-Sunday)

MCCOY'S REUNION

SE - Pikeville, downtown. (800) 844-7453. Light-hearted joking and fun surrounding the most famous feud in history. McCoys from all over the world and their invited guests (The Hatfields) will celebrate together. (2nd Saturday in June)

JEFFERSON DAVIS BIRTHDAY CELEBRATION

SW - Fairview, Jefferson Davis State Historic Site. (270) 886-1765. A living history celebration honors the Confederate President on his birthday at his birthplace. The 351 foot obelisk is the 4th tallest in the world with an elevator to the top for viewing. (1st weekend in June)

JULY

STEPHEN FOSTER-THE MUSICAL FOURTH OF JULY CELEBRATION

NC - Bardstown, My Old Kentucky Home SP. (800) 626-1563. Celebrate the birth of Foster, his music and our nation all in one night. (4th of July)

OFFICIAL KENTUCKY STATE CHAMPIONSHIP OLD TIME FIDDLER'S CONTEST

NC - Falls of Rough, Rough River Dam SRP. (270) 259-3578. 13 events including fiddle, harmonica, guitar, banjo and mandolin. (Next to last weekend in July)

"SALUTE TO THE NATION" WORLD WAR II BATTLE REENACTMENT

NC - Fort Knox, Patton Museum. (270) 352-1204. Authentic American and German Vehicles and Uniforms with an Army Band concert. (4th of July)

A SHAKER FOURTH

NC - Harrodsburg, Shaker Village of Pleasant Hill. (800) 734-5611. Celebrate the fourth in the old-time Shaker Way. (4th of July)

WATERFRONT INDEPENDENCE FESTIVAL

NC - Louisville, Waterfront Park/Slugger Field. (502) 574-3768 or www.louisvillewaterfront.com. Live music, a RiverBats baseball game, children's activities, festival food and fireworks extravaganza. (Around July 4th)

LIGHT UP SALT RIVER FESTIVAL

NC - Taylorsville. (502) 477-3246. Patriotic festival features a large fireworks display and the largest motorcycle rally (500 bikers) in KY. (1st Saturday in July)

SUMMER MOTION

NE - Ashland, Central Park and Riverfront. (800) 377-6249. 4th of July five day celebration is a huge party with fireworks, concerts, food, etc. (1st five days of July)

BLUEGRASS STATE GAMES

NE - Lexington. (859) 255-0336. Kentucky's premier amateur athletic competition for participants and spectators. (Mid-July weekend)

July (cont.)

4TH OF JULY FESTIVAL

NE - Lexington, downtown. (859) 258-3100. Patriotic music concert, race, parade, fireworks and entertainment.

NE - New Haven, Kentucky Railway Museum. (800) 272-0152.

NE - Versailles, Woodford County Park. (859) 873-8864.

NE - Wilmore. (859) 858-4411. Norman Rockwellesque small town celebration.

SUMMER FESTIVAL

NW - Owensboro, English Park. (800) 489-1131. The conclusion of this festival is the fireworks display with accompaniment by the Symphony. (3rd and 4th of July)

BALLOON CLASSIC

SC - Bowling Green. (270) 745-7509. Over 60 hot air balloons will fill the sky over town. (3rd or 4th weekend)

FOURTH OF JULY CELEBRATION

SC - Campbellsville. (270) 465-8601. Battlefield ceremony of markers.

NATIONAL CIVIL WAR BAND FESTIVAL

SC - Campbellsville University. (270) 789-5211. (Last weekend in July)

LAKEFEST

SC - Jamestown, Lake Cumberland. (270) 343-4594. Fun family festival. (1st weekend in July)

BEREA CRAFT AND INTERNATIONAL FOLK FESTIVALS

SE - Berea, throughout downtown and Indian Fort Theatre. (800) 598-5263. Voted the top 20 events in the southeast, there are usually over 125 artists from around the country demonstrating and selling their workmanship. International music, dance and theater are a wonderful compliment. (Mid-July weekend)

4TH OF JULY

SE - Berea. (859) 986-7710. Fireworks, kids activities, famous art demos of work in progress (years past it was sand art!).

SE - Richmond, Lake Reba Recreational Complex. (800) 866-3705.

FREEDOM FEST

SW - Murray. (800) 651-1603. Independence day with a community festival full of parades, concerts, fireworks and a street fair. (4th of July)

WESTERN KENTUCKY STATE FAIR

SW - Hopkinsville. (800) 842-9959. (Very end of July and 1st few days of August)

AUGUST

LIVING HISTORY AND CIVIL WAR SHOW

NC - Bardstown, Civil War Museum. (502) 349-0291. (1st full weekend in August)

<u>August (cont.)</u>

PIONEER DAYS

NC - Harrodsburg. (800) 355-9192. Kentucky's 1st settlement celebrates its history and heritage with food, square dancing, clogging, flint rock rifle shot contest and demonstrations. (3rd weekend in August)

KENTUCKY STATE FAIR

NC - Louisville, Kentucky Fair and Exposition Center. (502) 367-5000 or www.kyfairexpo.org. "Everybody's State Fair" offers over a dozen stages featuring many big name concerts, 10,000 animals, "thrillway" rides, World Championship Horse Show, senior and children's entertainment. (Mid-August to late-August for 11 days)

KIDS WEEKEND

NE - Lexington, KY Horse Park. (859) 233-4303. Admission $6-16. Beginners luck - hands-on with horses, treasure hunts, stick horse riding, horseshoe painting, children's horse shows, and storytelling. (1st full weekend in August)

BATTLE OF BLUE LICKS RE-ENACTMENT

NE - Mt. Olivet, Blue Licks Battlefield SRP. (859) 289-5507. The very last battle of the Revolutionary War is acted out with some light-hearted fun plus realistic living history. (3rd weekend in August)

STANTON CORN FESTIVAL

NE - Stanton, Stanton City Park. (606) 663-2271. Quaint corn festival with corn foods and music in the heart of the Red River Gorge.

AUGUST 8TH EMANCIPATION CELEBRATION

SW - Paducah. (800) PADUCAH. The town's African-American community celebrates with a memorial service, food, parade and lots of activity centers. (1st full week in August)

BATTLE OF MIDDLE CREEK

SE - Prestonsburg. (606) 886-1341. Future President James A. Garfield commanded the Union troops at this battle on January 10, 1862. It ended up being the largest battle in Eastern Kentucky. Technically a draw, but the Confederate troops retreated. See a re-enactment. (August)

SEPTEMBER

KENTUCKY FOLKLIFE FESTIVAL

NC - Frankfort, downtown. (502) 564-1792. Celebrate KY folklife with updated demonstrations and exhibits designed to educate and entertain visitors to KY culture, food and musical heritage. (Last weekend in September)

19TH CENTURY COUNTRY FAIR

NC - Harrodsburg, Shaker Village of Pleasant Hill. (800) 734-5611. Fall harvest event is reminiscent of an old time country fair. (4th weekend in September)

ANDERSON COUNTY BURGOO FESTIVAL

NC - Lawrenceburg. (502) 839-6959. A competition and tasting of the stew made with unusual and flavorful ingredients. "Everything but the kitchen sink" is the centerpiece of this tasty festival. (end of September and beginning of October weekend)

September (cont.)

ETHNIC FAIR

NC - **Louisville**, St. Michael Orthodox Church. (502) 454-3378. Food and music and dance and cultural displays from the Middle East, Greece, Russia and India. Rides and family activities both inside and outside. FREE. (Weekend after Labor Day)

WASHINGTON COUNTY SORGHUM FESTIVAL

NC - **Springfield**. (859) 336-3810. A fall harvest festival with agricultural products and farmers featured in areas of craft, food, and contests. (Late Sept., early October weekend)

OKTOBERFEST

NE - **Covington**, MainStrasse Village. (859) 491-0458. Fall celebration with traditional German accent on food and games. (Weekend after Labor Day)

HARVEST FESTIVAL

NE - **Georgetown**, Quest Farm. (502) 535-6064. Music, horseback riding, hayrides and good fall food. (2nd Sunday in September)

ROWAN COUNTY HARVEST FESTIVAL

NE - **Morehead**. (800) 654-1944. Celebrate the bountiful Kentucky harvest with bluegrass music, food, hayrides and train rides. (3rd weekend in September)

CAVE RUN STORYTELLING FESTIVAL

NE - **Morehead**. (800) 654-1944. Nationally known storytellers tell their tales in a scenic setting. (4th weekend in September)

MORGAN COUNTY SORGHUM FESTIVAL

NE – **Morgan County** Fairgrounds. (606) 743-3330. Mule-drawn cane mill, traditional food, craft demos, parade and live music. (4th weekend in September)

DANIEL BOONE PIONEER FESTIVAL

NE - **Winchester**, College Park. (800) 298-9105. Visit the Old Stone Church where the Boone's attended along with celebrating the Boone heritage with national entertainment, fireworks and a dance. (Labor Day weekend - Friday-Monday)

EVERLY BROTHERS HOMECOMING

NW - **Central City**. (270) 754-2360. Don and Phil Everly host a grand concert. Bring lawn chairs and blankets. (Labor Day Saturday)

BROMER'S APPLE FARM & CIDER MILL

SC - **Bowling Green**, 101 Claypool-Alvaton Road (corner KY 234 & 961). http://members.aol.com/bappfarm/bromer.htm. (270) 782-9243 or Drive out to the country to purchase freshly picked apples or warm fried apple pie or fresh squeezed apple cider. Pick-u-own and special weekends with apple themes. (entire month of September)

CASEY COUNTY APPLE FESTIVAL

SC - **Casey County** Fairgrounds. www.theapplefestival.com. (606) 787-8177. The world's largest apple pie is complemented by a parade, apple foods, music, contests and fireworks. (very last weekend in September)

September (cont.)

CONSTITUTION SQUARE FESTIVAL

SC - Danville, Constitution Square State Historical Site, downtown. (859) 239-7089. Celebrate where Kentucky's Statehood began with a visit to the 1st Post Office west of the Alleghenies, a jail, the courthouse and the meeting house. The site is set up as life was 200 years ago with arts and crafts demos, living history actors and entertainment. (3rd weekend in September)

MARION COUNTY COUNTRY HAM DAYS

SC - Lebanon. (270) 692-9594 or www.hamdays.com. Over 600 hams are prepared to serve with Southern style side dishes. Cloggers, line dances, steam engine show, Pokey Pig Run and entertainment. (4th weekend in September)

MONROE COUNTY WATERMELON FESTIVAL

SC - Monroe County Fairgrounds. (270) 487-5504. Rolley-hole Marble (hand-made flint) tournaments, watermelon-related competitions, live music and a street dance. (Labor Day Saturday)

SPOONBREAD FESTIVAL

SE - Berea. (859) 986-9760. This festival honors the famous bread served at Boone Tavern. Check out the spoonbread eating contest, live music, children's activities, food and hot air balloons. (2nd weekend in September)

BLACK GOLD FESTIVAL

SE - Hazard. (606) 436-0161. Coal is honored with amusements, great mountain food, a parade and a coal truck competition. (Mid-September)

BREATHITT COUNTY HONEY FESTIVAL

SE - Jackson. (606) 666-7414. The mountain hamlet is abuzz with a Honey Bowl, parade, baking contest and food made with honey. (Labor Day Weekend)

WORLD CHICKEN FESTIVAL

SE - London, downtown. www.chickenfestival.com. (800) 348-0095 or You are egg-spected for this good time complete with a gander at the World's Largest Skillet, entertainment and rides. It celebrates the county where the 1st Kentucky Fried Chicken was established. Come with an appetite! (4th weekend in September - Thursday-Sunday)

TRAIL OF TEARS INDIAN POW-WOW

SW - Hopkinsville, Trail of Tears Park (US 41/9th St. & Skyline Drive). (800) 842-9959. A sad period in our country's history is remembered with tribal dancing, Native American storytelling and food. Meet Chiefs Whitepath and Fly Smith and stop in the Heritage Museum (open Tuesday-Saturday 10am-2pm year round) to view cultural displays. (Weekend after Labor Day)

OFFICIAL KENTUCKY LABOR DAY PARADE

SW - Paducah. (800) PADUCAH. Celebration includes live entertainment, a barbeque and the parade. (Labor Day weekend)

WESTERN KENTUCKY HIGHLAND FESTIVAL

SW – Paducah, Carson Park Fairgrounds. (270) 443-2064. Celebrate the Celtic heritage with pipe and drum bands, dancers, athletes, and children's activities. (2nd Saturday in September)

September (cont.)

ANTIQUE GAS AND STEAM ENGINE SHOW

SW – Paducah, Carson Park. (270) 554-1282. Antique cars, tractors and engines, tractor pulls, wheat threshing, pulling teams, parades, arts & crafts, barbecue and music. (3rd weekend in September)

SEPTEMBER / OCTOBER

AUTUMNFEST

NE - Georgetown, Bi-Water Farm (US 25N). (502) 863-3676. Farm festival full of color and fall food and hayrides. (4th weekend in September thru October)

FESTIVAL OF THE HORSE

NE - Georgetown. (502) 863-2547. Central Kentucky's premiere horse festival with a family orientation featuring entertainment, food, a children's parade and of course, a horse show. (End of Sept., beginning of Oct. weekend)

PUMPKIN FEST

NE - Georgetown, Double Stink Hog Farm (I-75exit 126, US 460E & KY 922). (502) 868-9703. A festival famous for their down-home country festivals with u-pick pumpkins, food, a petting zoo and hayrides. (Last weekend in September and 1st weekend in October)

CARTER COUNTY SORGHUM FESTIVAL

NE - Grayson. (606) 474-4003. A harvest farm festival where the old cane mill is running, turning raw plant into sticky sweet sorghum. Music and food add to the farm setting charm. (Late Sept., early Oct. weekend)

PUMPKIN FESTIVAL

NE - **Maysville**, "R" Farm, 7172 Strodes Run Rd. (606) 742-2429. (Last weekend in Sept., 1st weekend in October)

CUMBERLAND MOUNTAIN FALL FESTIVAL

SE - Middlesboro and Cumberland Gap NHP. (800) 988-1075 or www.thefallfestival.com. Old English pioneer heritage through the gap is celebrated with live pioneer demos, crafts, food and entertainment. (late Sept., early Oct. weekend)

OCTOBER

RED CROW INDIAN COUNCIL'S DAYS

NC - **Bardstown**, Nelson County Fairgrounds. (800) 638-4877. A traditional Indian gathering with dancers in regalia, demos and food. (3rd weekend in October)

WATSON'S PUMPKIN PATCH FESTIVAL

NC - **Bardstown**, Watson's Farm. (502) 252-7212. Fall favorites like hayrides, a hay maze, carnival rides, sorghum making, homemade food and pony rides. (1st full weekend in October)

TWO RIVERS FESTIVAL

NC - **Carrollton**, confluence of the KY and OH Rivers. (502) 732-5713. Fall festival with all of a rivertown flare. (1st weekend in October)

GREAT PUMPKIN FESTIVAL

NC - **Frankfort**. (502) 223-2261. Harvest season with hayrides, children's activities, costume parade down Main Street, pumpkin decorating and live entertainment. (3rd weekend in October)

October (cont.)

LINCOLN DAYS CELEBRATION

NC - Hodgenville. (270) 358-3411. Honoring native son Abraham Lincoln with a Lincoln Look Alike and Mary Todd Lincoln contests, antique costume contests, pioneer games and railsplitting tournaments. (2nd weekend in October)

RIVERSIDE HERITAGE FESTIVAL

NC - Louisville, Riverside-The Farnsley-Moremen Landing. (502) 935-6809. A good time to visit this historic home with children as fun activities like crafts, food and river boat rides are offered. (2nd Sunday in October)

COLORFEST

NC - Louisville, Bernheim Forest. (502) 955-8512. Fall festival featuring craft and nature exhibits for children, food, storytelling, music and activities. (3rd weekend in October)

KENTUCKY WOOL FESTIVAL

NE - Falmouth. (859) 654-3378. Once a strong area sheep industry town, now the area maintains its heritage with demos on sheep shearing and sheep dog herding, wool spinning, sorghum and corn products, ethnic foods and a petting zoo. (2nd weekend in October)

BIG BONE LICK SALT FESTIVAL

NE - Union, Big Bone Lick SP. (859) 384-3522. A festival devoted to exploring the significance of area salt licks to early pioneers with demos and crafts. (3rd weekend in October)

APPLE FESTIVAL

NW - Owensboro, Reid's Orchard (KY 144). (270) 685-2444. An abundance of apples are featured in a carnival, crafts, pick-u-own and apple food and cider. (3rd weekend in October)

PUMPKIN FESTIVAL

SC - Edmonton. (270) 432-3561. Area grown prize pumpkins are weighed, carved and cooked to make fall crafts and food. (1st Saturday in October)

GREAT OUTHOUSE BLOWOUT

SC – Gravel Switch, Penn's Store. (859) 332-7715. The annual memorial tribute to the 1992 Penn's Privy Dedication (gained national attention the year they first installed an outhouse). Featuring the "Outhouse 300" where teams race the 300 foot course, pushing and pulling their "designer outhouses" on wheels for the "gold" in outhouse racing. Also see the Parade of Privies, music, outhouse memorabilia and great food. Fee for parking. (1st Saturday in October)

COLORFALL

SC - Mammoth Cave National Park. (270) 726-2254. A wonderful addition to your family "cave" experience celebrating the cultural heritage of this region with storytelling and archeological demos. (2nd week in October)

PERRYVILLE BATTLEFIELD COMMEMORATION

SC - Perryville Battlefield SHS. (859) 332-8631. Living history exhibits and battle re-enactments honor the worst of Kentucky's Civil War battles with encampments, sutters and music. Parking fee. (1st full weekend in October)

October (cont.)

HARVEST FESTIVAL

SC - Russell Springs. (270) 343-3191. Fall harvest-time is here and the area's fresh produce is displayed and sold here along with fall crafts, food and entertainment. (1st Saturday in October)

LEE COUNTY WOLLY WORM FESTIVAL

SE - Beattyville. (606) 464-2888. A unique annual celebration of the predictor of coming winter weather with announcement of results of a survey sent to the National Weather Service along with crafts, entertainment and a wolly worm race (as the fans cheer them on!). (3rd weekend in October)

CAMP WILDCAT RE-ENACTMENT

SE - London, Wildcat Mountain. (606) 528-1817. The Civil War battle of Wildcat is re-enacted as the 1st Union victory of the War (along Wilderness Road) with living history exhibits. (3rd weekend in October)

KENTUCKY APPLE FESTIVAL

SE - Paintsville. (800) 542-5790. The orchards are harvested and the products honored with apple foods and crafts, amusement rides, a parade, square dancing and clogging and live entertainment. (1st Saturday in October)

KIDSDAYS

SE - Richmond, Lake Reba Recreation Complex. (800) 866-3705. A carnival and activities totally devoted to kids having fun. (2nd long weekend in October, Weds-Sun)

APPALACHIAN HARVEST FESTIVAL

SE - Renfro Valley. (800) 765-7464. Fall harvest-time with an old fashioned flare including molasses made from a mule-drawn press, antique farm machinery, music and a covered-wagon train. (1st weekend in October)

FIDDLERS FESTIVAL

SE - Renfro Valley. (800) 765-7464. Toe-tapping fun as fiddlers from around the country get together to perform and just jam. (last weekend in October)

CIVIL WAR DAYS

SW - Columbus, Columbus-Belmont SP. (270) 677-2327. The living history presentations portray Grant's 1st assignment at a strategic location for control of the Mississippi River. They formed a Confederate "chain of men" and this is re-enacted. (2nd weekend in October)

FESTIVAL OF MURALS AND ARTS IN ACTION

SW - Paducah. (800) PADUCAH. Paducah celebrates its history as the floodwall murals are "brought to life" in living history performances. Demonstrating artists, arts and crafts sales, live music and dance performances, games, hay rides, Taste of Paducah, free museum and gallery admission. (2nd Saturday in October)

NOVEMBER

FT. HARROD HOLIDAY GALA

NC - Harrodsburg, Old Ft. Harrod SP. (859) 734-3314. A Victorian open house celebration with a Christmas tree festival and Mr. & Mrs. Claus. (3rd weekend in November)

November (cont.)

LIGHT UP LOUISVILLE

NC – Louisville. Jefferson Square. (502) 568-7000. The switch is thrown at dusk (~7:40pm) to illuminate downtown with over 40 buildings covered in holiday lights. There's also Santa's arrival, fireworks, a global village, entertainment throughout the day, and a children's holiday parade in the daytime. (Day after Thanksgiving)

NOVEMBER / DECEMBER

SANTA EXPRESS

Train rides with Santa and treats.

NC - New Haven, Kentucky Railway Museum. (800) 272-0152 (Thanksgiving weekend and every weekend until mid-December)

NE - Versailles, Bluegrass Scenic RR. (800) 755-2476. (Thanksgiving-December)

CHRISTMAS OPEN HOUSES

A great family time to visit many elaborate homes that may be too stuffy or boring to tour (for kids) any other time of year. Open houses generally have extensive holiday decorations, music and refreshments served. Admission is charged.

- ❑ **NC - Bardstown**, My Old Kentucky Home. (800) 323-7803. Candlelight tours with elaborate period costumes and horse-drawn carriages. (Thanksgiving-2nd Saturday in December)
- ❑ **NC - Louisville**, Riverside, the Farnsley-Moremen Landing. (502) 935-6809. (1st Saturday in December)
- ❑ **NE – Burlington**, Dinsmore Farm. (859)586-6117 or www.dinsmorefarm.org. (1ST Long full weekend in December)

❑ **NE - Lexington**, Ashland, Henry Clay Estate. (859) 266-8581. Civil War Christmas. (Day after Thanksgiving - December)

❑ **NE - Lexington**, Waveland SHS. (859) 272-3611. (1st ten days in December)

❑ **SC - Bowling Green**, Riverview at Hobson Grove. (270) 843-5565. Southern KY Victorian style tours. (Last week of Nov - just before Christmas)

❑ **SC - Danville**, McDowell House. (800) 755-0076. (1st full weekend in December)

FESTIVAL OF LIGHTS

❑ **NC - Leitchfield**, Holiday Lights Driving Tour and Home Tours. (888) 624-9957. (December)

❑ **NC - Louisville**, Festival of Trees and Lights. (502) 629-8052. (Thanksgiving-time thru December)

❑ **NE - Ashland**, Winter Wonderland of Lights. (800) 377-6249 or www.winterwonderland.org. 700,000 plus lights of 35 displays seen by carriage ride through community with centerpiece at Central Park.

❑ **NE - Lexington**, Southern Lights, Kentucky Horse Park. (800) 678-8813. With the Horse Park setting, drive thru 2.5 miles of animated displays of lighted holiday cartoon characters, many equine-themed action scenes, Cinderella's carriage and dinosaurs. Santa, mini-trains, performers, snacks and hot beverages are available too. Nightly 5:30-10:00pm. Admission per carload approx. $12. (Saturday before Thanksgiving - December)

❑ **NE - Mt. Sterling**, Christmas in the Park, Easy Walker Park. (859) 498-3800. A walking tour of a park aglow with over 85 decorated trees and 10,000 lights. (week of Thanksgiving - New Year's Day)

❑ **SC - Bowling Green**, Winter Lights, Basil Griffin Park. (270) 782-3660. Car drive thru huge light displays. (late November - New Year's Eve)

❑ **SC - Burnside**, Christmas Island, General Burnside Island SP. (800) 642-6287. One million lights on this 3.5 mile tour through a wonderland of 300 lighted displays. Horse-drawn carriage rides. (weekend before Thanksgiving - day before New Year's Eve)

Festival Of Lights (cont.)

❑   **SE - Hazard**, Christmas in Perry County Park. (606) 439-2659.
    Drive-through of wonderful lights that make the town look like
    the North Pole. (Thanksgiving-time - Christmas Day)
❑   **SE - Renfro Valley**, Christmas in the Valley. (800) 765-7464.
    One of KY's largest light displays, performances and special
    holiday shopping. (weekend before Thanksgiving - mid
    December)
❑   **SE - Richmond**, Hummel Planetarium, Story of A Star. (859)
    622-1547. (Thanksgiving weekend - December)

DECEMBER

CHRISTMAS PARADES

❑   **NE - Versailles**. (859) 873-5436. 1st Saturday in December.
❑   **NW - Marion**. (270) 965-5015. 2nd Saturday in December.
❑   **SW - Paducah**. (800) PADUCAH. 1st Saturday in December.
❑   **SC - Bradfordsville**. (502) 337-2085. 1st Saturday in December.
❑   **SC - Edmonton**. (270) 432-3222. 2nd Saturday in December.
❑   **SC - Lebanon Junction**. (502) 833-2296. 2nd Saturday in
    December.
❑   **SC - Somerset**. (606) 679-7323. 1st Saturday in December.
❑   **SE - London**, downtown. (606) 864-4789. 1st Saturday in
    December.
❑   **SE - Richmond**. (800) 866-3705. 1st weekend in December.
❑   **SE - Harlan**. (606) 573-4717. 1st Saturday in December.

BETHLEHEM LIVING NATIVITY

NC - Bethlehem. (502) 845-5046. A still scene depicting the
Christmas story with live characters and animals. (4 days before
and including Christmas)

SHAKER ORDER OF CHRISTMAS

NC - Harrodsburg, Shaker Village of Pleasant Hill. Partake in viewing Shaker traditions in music and decorations and community caroling. (1st full week in December beginning Saturday)

CAPTAIN SANTA CRUISE

NC - Louisville, Spirit of Jefferson. (502) 574-2355. Games, dancing, and high energy fun with hosts Elf Mary and Santa. Admission $8-$12. (first three Saturday mornings in December)

CHRISTMAS ON THE FARM

NE - Corinth, Mullins Log Cabin. (859) 824-4306. An old-fashioned country gathering with craft demos and wagon rides and warm food. (1st weekend in December)

NEW YEARS EVE CELEBRATIONS

No alcohol, "First Night" themed, family-friendly evening activities and party with live entertainment all the way past midnight!

- ❑ **State Resort Parks**. (800) 225-PARK. Reservations needed.
- ❑ **NE - Ashland**, Judd Plaza. (800) 377-6249.
- ❑ **NW - Owensboro**. (502) 687-8700.

**WEST CLINTON
MENNONITE CHURCH**

NOTES

NOTES

NOTES

NOTES

GROUP DISCOUNTS & FUNDRAISING OPPORTUNITIES!

Dear Coordinator:

We're excited to introduce our books to your group! These guides for parents, grandparents, teachers and visitors are great tools to help you discover hundreds of fun places to visit. **KIDS ♥ PUBLICATIONS** titles are great resources for all the wonderful places to travel either locally or across the region.

We are two parents who have researched, written and published these books. We have spent thousands of hours collecting information and *personally traveled over 10,000 miles* visiting all of the most unique places listed in our guides. The books are kid-tested and the descriptions include great hints on what kids like best!

Please consider the following Group Purchase options: *For the latest information, visit our website:* **www.kidslovepublications.com**

❑ **Group Discount/Fundraising** – Purchase books at the price of $10.00 each and offer the (~25%) savings off the suggested retail price to members/friends. Minimum order is ten books. You may mix titles to reach the minimum order. Greater discounts (~35%) are available for fundraisers. Call for details.

❑ **Available for Interview/Speaking** – The authors have a treasure bag full of souvenirs from favorite places. We'd love to share ideas on planning fun trips to take children while exploring your home state. The authors are available, by appointment, at (614) 792-6451. The minimum guaranteed order is: 30 books in Ohio, 50 books for other states. There is no additional fee involved.

Call us soon at (614) 792-6451 to make arrangements!
Happy Exploring!

Attention Parents:

All titles are "Kid Tested". *The authors and kids personally visited all of the most unique places* and wrote the books with warmth and excitement from a parent's perspective. Find tried and true places that children will enjoy. No more boring trips! Listings provide: Names, addresses, telephone numbers, <u>websites</u> (*except Kids Love Indiana*), directions, and descriptions. All books include a <u>bonus chapter</u> listing state-wide kid-friendly Seasonal & Special Events!

KIDS LOVE INDIANA ™

❖ **Discover places where you can "co-star" in a cartoon or climb a giant sand dune.** Almost 600 listings in one book about Indiana travel. 10 geographical zones, 193 pages.

KIDS LOVE KENTUCKY ™

❖ **Discover places from Boone to Burgoo, from Caves to Corvettes, and from Lincoln to the Lands of Horses.** Over 500 listings in one book about Kentucky travel. 6 geographic zones. 224 pages.

KIDS LOVE MICHIGAN ™

❖ **Discover places where you can "race" over giant sand dunes, climb aboard a lighthouse "ship", eat at the world's largest breakfast table, or watch yummy foods being made.** Almost 600 listings in one book about Michigan travel. 8 geographical zones, 237 pages.

KIDS LOVE OHIO ™

❖ **Discover places like hidden castles and whistle factories.** Almost 1000 listings in one book about Ohio travel. 9 geographical zones, 257 pages.

KIDS LOVE PENNSYLVANIA ™

❖ **Explore places where you can "discover" oil and coal, meet Ben Franklin, or watch you favorite toys and delicious, fresh snacks being made.** Over 900 listings in one book about Pennsylvania travel. 9 geographical zones, 268 pages.

KIDS LOVE TRAVEL MEMORIES ™

❖ Be sure to check out our website at: **www.kidslovepublications.com** for the perfect scrapbook companion to our books!

ORDER FORM

KIDS LOVE PUBLICATIONS

7438 Sawmill Road, # 500
Columbus, OH 43235
(614) 792-6451
Visit our website: **www.kidslovepublications.com**

#	Title		Price	Total
	Kids Love Indiana		$12.95	
	Kids Love Michigan		$12.95	
	Kids Love Pennsylvania		$12.95	
	Kids Love Ohio		$13.95	
	Kids Love Kentucky		$13.95	
COMBO PRICING – INDICATE TITLES ABOVE				
	Combo #2 - Any 2 Titles		$21.95	
	Combo #3 - Any 3 Titles		$29.95	
	Combo #4 - Any 4 Titles		$36.95	
	Combo #5 - All 5 Titles		$43.95	

		Subtotal	
Note: All combo pricing is for different titles only . For multiple copies (10+) of one title, please call or visit our website for volume discounts.	(Ohio Residents Only) $1.00 per book	Sales Tax	
		Shipping	
		TOTAL	

[] Master Card   [] Visa

Account Number _ _ _ _ - _ _ _ _ - _ _ _ _ - _ _ _ _
Exp Date: _ _ / _ _ (Month/Year)
Cardholder's Name _____
Signature *(required)* _____

(Please make check or money order payable to: KIDS LOVE PUBLICATIONS)

Name: _____
Address:_____
City:_____State:_____
Zip:_____Telephone:_____

All orders are shipped within 2 business days of receipt by US Mail or Fed-X Ground. Your satisfaction is 100% guaranteed or simply return your order for a prompt refund. Thanks for your order!